*Draw your chair up close to the edge of the precipice,
and I will tell you a story.*

F. SCOTT FITZGERALD, *THE CRACK-UP*

*I will give you the treasures of darkness
and riches hidden in secret places,
With honey from the rock I [will] satisfy you.
You shall be called the repairer of the breach,
the restorer of streets to live in.*

ISAIAH 45:3; PSALM 81:16; ISAIAH 58:12 NRSV

stone CROSSINGS

Finding Grace in Hard and Hidden Places

L. L. Barkat

IVP Books

An imprint of InterVarsity Press
Downers Grove, Illinois

InterVarsity Press
P.O. Box 1400, Downers Grove, IL 60515-1426
World Wide Web: www.ivpress.com
E-mail: email@ivpress.com

InterVarsity Press® *is the book-publishing division of InterVarsity Christian Fellowship/USA*®*, a student movement active on campus at hundreds of universities, colleges and schools of nursing in the United States of America, and a member movement of the International Fellowship of Evangelical Students. For information about local and regional activities, write Public Relations Dept., InterVarsity Christian Fellowship/USA, 6400 Schroeder Rd., P.O. Box 7895, Madison, WI 53707-7895, or visit the IVCF website at <www.intervarsity.org>.*

All Scripture quotations, unless otherwise indicated, are taken from the Holy Bible, New International Version®. NIV®. *Copyright* ©*1973, 1978, 1984 by International Bible Society. Used by permission of Zondervan Publishing House. All rights reserved.*

The poem "Fire by Fire" by Madeleine L'Engle cited in chapter 15 is taken from The Weather of the Heart *(Wheaton, Ill: H. Shaw, 1978). Used with permission.*

The poem "Community Life" in chapter 20 is used with permission of Bill McConnell.

Design: Rebecca Larson
Images: Craig Brewer/Getty Images

ISBN 978-0-8308-3495-2

Printed in the United States of America ∞

Library of Congress Cataloging-in-Publication Data

Barkat, L. L., 1964-
    Stone crossings: finding grace in hard and hidden places/L.L. Barkat
    p. cm.
    Includes bibliographical references.
    ISBN 978-0-8308-3495-2 (pbk.: alk. paper)
    1. Spirituality. 2. Grace (Theology) I. Title.
    BV4501.3.B365 2008
    242—dc22

                                                        2007049468

| **P** | 14 | 13 | 12 | 11 | 10 | 9 | 8 | 7 | 6 | 5 | 4 | 3 | 2 | 1 |
| **Y** | 19 | 18 | 17 | 16 | 15 | 14 | 13 | 12 | 11 | 10 | 09 | 08 |

To my mother and father

contents

acknowledgments

Thanks to my editor, Cindy Bunch, who wisely suspected when there was more to the story and inspired me to set the truth free. You've been a gentle and welcome companion. Deep thanks go to my mother and father and my stepmother, Beezie, who let me tell their stories, painful and unflattering as they sometimes were, for the sake of others who need hope and healing. To my dear husband, John, who gently told me it was time to embrace the writing life, much appreciation. J, you've given me all I needed, and more, to take this journey—grace, love, laughter, the occasional much-needed reality check, and more evenings and Saturdays to myself than I can count.

Thanks also to Mom and Dad Barkat. Your prayers and blessings were a quiet gift that brought great strength in the midst of an arduous process. To my church and to the WTW ministry, thanks for giving me some of my first platforms to stand on and for cultivating in me an immeasurable love and respect for the Scriptures. To all my friends who put up with my absence and the changes in my life, and to some who even read the manuscript when it was still in pieces, much appreciation. Thanks also to my precious sister, Sandi, who lived the long-ago dark days with me and encouraged me as I put them back together for others to see. You are the better writer, and I hope someday you'll grace the world with your own amazing stories.

Much love to my dear children Sara and Sonia, whose lives I am blessed to shepherd. I thank God for you—so deeply you'll never know, and I pray that you'll grow to be women who bring much-needed grace to this troubled world. Lastly, thanks to my Abba God: "Great are thy tender mercies" (Psalm 119:156 KJV).

1

stepping stones ~ conversion

As a child, I escape into the creek bed. No one can touch me here. It is a haven where I curl my bare, sun-browned toes into wet clay. I am hidden at the base of a ravine. The ravine has, on one side, exposed roots that hang in thin air or cling to stone and crumbling earth. On the other side, a vast forest slumbers over needle-feathered bronze. At my feet, a silver-green ribbon winds and disappears past ancient tangles of swaying firs. I wonder how long the creek has been here to cut a path so deep, to dig this secret place where water babbles to bending reeds and crystal fish dart from shadow to shadow. Ready to explore, I pick my first stepping stone and leave the muddy shore behind. All day I leap from rock to rock—sometimes backtracking from a dead-end stone, sometimes slipping and scraping my naked knee, sometimes resting. Intrigued and comforted, I want to stay here forever. Ask me where I first stepped in and I may not remember, nor hardly care. I would rather pluck a pebble from the creek bed and show you the crayfish hiding under a web of sticks.

The haven of my pebbled creek is long lost. Buried in a childhood past. But I remember it the way I remember stepping into faith—with all the urgency and hope we feel when we think about beginnings and where they have since taken us . . .

I came to God through a want ad. "Piano for sale," it said.

My flame-haired stepmother, Beryl (or Beezie, as we called her), ran the ad because somebody left a baby grand in Boston. This oversized piano stood in the living room of the home Beezie and my father had just bought, a good four hours from me, my sister and our creek. The abandoned baby grand, plus two pianos we already owned, left us with three oversized instruments—a trinity, if you will, which is a special number.

Now some of us put a lot of stock in special numbers. But special numbers didn't mean a thing to Beezie or my father, especially if the numbers were supposedly spiritual. Indeed, my father had some choice words he reserved to describe superstitions, fairy tales and Jesus Christ. And Beezie, well, when it came to discussions of anything spiritual, she told stories about parochial school in the hushed whispers of one who is both angry and hopelessly sad. Nothing as simple as the spiritual number three was going to change things in their house.

Yet with the purchase of a new home, we suddenly had three pianos. And nobody needs more pianos than bathrooms, even if they are easier to clean. So the number three propelled Beezie to sell one of our pianos in the want ads. Little did she know. For divine providence was about to have some fun by putting Beezie's ad into the hands of Opal Bonesteel, a charismatic Christian with a capital C—who, incidentally, had considered buying that same

Boston home but had settled for praying for its future owners room by room. You could say that Opal was God's cosmic mischief let loose in my father's house.

Opal looked like her name. She had silver hair that puffed out round, and she used a great deal of Mary Kay, which gave her face a rosy glow. Her pearly teeth shone every time she threw her head back to shout, "Praise the Lord!" I'm not sure why my stepmother didn't just quietly close the door in her face when Opal showed up to see the piano. If Beezie had wanted to remain a Catholic-gone-bad, she really shouldn't have let Opal into the house.

Certainly, if my atheist father had been home, he would have known to bar the door. Unfortunately for him, God knows the details of our schedules—like when we're on a business trip, out at a hockey game or even off sneaking doughnuts. So he knew just when to send Opal.

Actually, I suspect he knew more than when to send her. He also knew why to send her. Opal was one of those people who actually read her Bible and believed it. I imagine she cherished all those stories of unlikely conversions—like Naaman, for instance, a Syrian military commander and enemy of Israel who came to the prophet Elisha to be healed of leprosy. Naaman had a good life but he lacked good looks. Without plastic surgeons or pharmaceutical options, he was doomed to suffer the discomfort of perpetual disfigurement. Then he heard about the prophet of the Lord and went to Samaria to seek healing.

After some disagreements with the prophet and a tantrum over God's healing plan, Naaman went along with God's instructions and washed in the Jordan. Finding himself restored, he declared,

"Now I know that there is no God in all the earth except in Israel" (2 Kings 5:15 NRSV).

I think Opal knew all about Naaman, along with Rahab, Jacob and Paul—the hard cases, the unlikely ones: prostitutes, deceivers and murderers who turned out to be parents of saviors, nations and churches. Mostly, though, it strikes me that Opal knew about God. It was like she could hear him humming, "When Israel was a child, I loved him, / and out of Egypt I called my son. / . . . It was I who taught Ephraim to walk, / taking them by the arms" (Hosea 11:1-3).

Opal's belief that God could take any hand and woo any heart—even a wounded and angry one—became a comfort to Beezie, who found Jesus beside the piano. But it confused my father. That day after Opal came, he lost his biker babe and found, in her place, a Bible babe standing in his very own kitchen. She was cooking something innocent like macaroni and cheese and was quietly planning to lead his children to the Lord.

It's my theory that some people, when they're spiritually confused and threatened, open their cuss-word encyclopedia and use the words therein to beat down anyone who senses their fear and confusion. My father was a classic case. That day in the kitchen he immediately sensed a change. The only leather his biker babe was sporting sat prim and proper on the back of her new King James. He was furious.

So my father attacked Beezie with a lot of special-edition words, and then he made a serious miscalculation in his strategy to banish God from the house. He ranted against the Bible with all the fervor of a Pentecostal preacher: "I'm going to read this piece of sh—t and prove that this book of fairy tales is nothing but a pack of Jewish lies!" Then he thumped his fist on the poor King James.

See, my father forgot how fairy tales end. Over the next months he read the Bible, cussing all the way, thinking he was proving God didn't exist. Then he got to the history stuff, the predictive prophecy and Middle East stuff—Isaiah, to be exact. The truths he encountered resonated with my father's broad knowledge of geography and history. Suddenly, impossibly, it was happily ever after for my father. Imagine our surprise when he came slinking to his new Bible babe and admitted that there is no God in all the earth except in Israel.

Beezie took this turn of events as blatant permission to share God with her son, my sister and me. She presented the gospel to us one summer day, over peanut butter and Fluffernutter sandwiches on white bread. At bedtime we prayed the sinner's prayer.

Now if I wanted to be eligible for testimony of the year, this would be a good place to stop. My story reveals an obvious stepping stone into faith. But as Malcolm Muggeridge has pointed out, even blatant conversions are not so elegantly simple. In fact, many people cannot even pinpoint a specific stepping stone, as growth into faith is an intricate process.

Nevertheless, having attended a Christian college where everyone had a ready testimony, I decided long ago to settle on the story I just told. This is the testimony I've had in my pocket in case anybody popped the question, "So how did you become a Christian?" But the truth is, I'm not comfortable with this story any longer. It's a little too short and sweet.

That's why, if you asked me today how I became a Christian, I would show you the picture that's already on the table—of my father and Beezie and a shimmering lady named Opal Bonesteel. Then I'd take you back to the muddy banks of my stepfather's home, to a time I've spent most of my life trying to forget.

There, in a hard and hidden place, informed by God's Word— his "treasures of darkness and riches hidden in secret places"—we would begin our journey through a stream of grace that redeems the past, challenges the present and shapes a vision for the future.

So here it is. I'm game to explore if you are. Just let me take off my shoes.

2

CHRISTMAS COAL ~ SHAME

By Christmas, the creek we love to play in has long been frozen. The softness of moss-covered rocks, the solace of sun-baked stones lie submerged in aqua ice. We can no longer walk beneath the fragrant pines, for the forest floor is buried in drifts that rise to our middles. We move indoors. Here the scent of spruce rises from our gilded tree; it pushes against the stale odor of cigarette and drifts through voices that often speak in dirty syllables—words I hide from with all my strength. Yet tonight, in the sparkle of Christmas lights, the voices speak kindly to me. My stepfather smiles and says, "Go look in your Christmas stocking. Santa came early."

"Yes, he came early," echo the voices of his sons. These men, these voices, herd me toward the stocking. I look up to my mother. I look up to eyes of the men. It's clear that the stocking holds a slender item, waiting for me.

I still remember the night my stepfather invited me to reach into that stocking—how I fumbled into the crimson velvet only to bring to light a lone feminine product. Finding this object was

worse than receiving a lump of stony coal. I stood in the center of
those laughing men, a child of nine years old, and my heart turned
to wax. I would have given anything to be a moth and flutter into
darkness. There was nowhere to hide.

These feelings of wanting to hide, to flee, were familiar to me at
that point in life. Familiar because of repeated emotional exposures
like the one I experienced that Christmas night. Familiar because
of a season of molestation in my stepfather's house. And familiar
too because of my own childish missteps. (I still remember, for
instance, when I stole a chocolate bar from a store and couldn't
hide the sin from my mother. When she noticed the evidence, I
wanted to crawl under a grocery cart, and when she made me go
pay the cashier with chocolate-stained fingers, I thought I'd rather
die than set things right.)

In my early years it seemed good to cover up such shameful family and personal secrets. Everyone else appeared to be untouched,
free of chocolate fingerprints and hidden wrappers. This reminds
me of a story I once heard Walter Wangerin tell. Wangerin grew up
with a mother who alternately loved and abused him. One day she
tied Walter and his brother into potato sacks and set them at the
curb. As the garbage truck came barreling down the street, a neighbor happened to notice two talking sacks and said, "Did that
Wangerin woman put her boys in those potato sacks?" Walter was
quick to shout, "You bet she did, and she was right to do it!"

Shame is not easy to bear, and like me, like Wangerin, people
have an instinct to cover it up. Yet we must also come to terms
with it—which is why, I suspect, the Bible tells a shame story as
early as chapter three. Surely the writer of Genesis could have gone

on a little longer about the glories of creation, but instead he sets a tale of disgrace right at the beginning, as if telling us that, yes, shame is a big deal and we've got to face it at the outset.

As we remember, the story unfolds like this: Adam and Eve eat a forbidden fruit; assailed by guilt, they cover up and hide. Soon God calls, "Where are you?" and the man answers, "I heard you in the garden, and I was afraid because I was naked; so I hid" (Genesis 3:10). Adam's response billows with shame in its details: the cold fear, hiding at the sound of footsteps, reaching for fig leaves before his nakedness can be discovered.

It seems that Adam felt like I used to feel—that it would be comforting to hide in darkness, that it would be a relief to flee from the God who walks around knowing what I've been up to. Yet to get away, Adam would have had to remove God from the garden or revoke God's license to know: "Before him no creature is hidden, but all are naked and laid bare" (Hebrews 4:13 NRSV); "There is nothing hidden that will not be disclosed, and nothing concealed that will not be known or brought out into the open" (Luke 8:17). Of course, Adam could not make such adjustments.

But life in my society feels different. I live in a place that often blots God from the universe, maybe because it's so frightening to face our shameful feelings. Yet if we want to erase the idea of a God who sees our shameful actions, who calls us to account, we bump into problems that are equally frightening.

I like the way a Flannery O'Connor character explores this: "If [Jesus] did what He said, then it's nothing for you to do but throw away everything to follow Him, and if He didn't, then it's nothing for you to do but enjoy the few minutes you got left the best way you can—by killing somebody or burning down his house or doing some other meanness to him."

The character tells it straight: if God isn't God, if he's absent or doesn't see, then people's shameful actions don't really matter. My stolen chocolate bar didn't matter. Wangerin's mother's abuse didn't matter. My stepfather's malice at Christmas and every other day of the year didn't matter. Yet how unsatisfying such "freedom" would be.

Instead I take comfort in what I ultimately believe: that the shame highlighted in Genesis stems from a nagging feeling that God is walking in the garden, seeing the things we've been up to, and that we need some major fig leaves—maybe even the whole darn tree. Of course, this comfort can be hard to come by when we first try to step into God's presence.

My sister recently reminded me that she'd had a hard time entering God's presence at first because of her shame. "I knew I was doing wrong," she told me. "I didn't feel I could come to God. I was too ashamed." I asked her what changed things, and her response surprised me. "Don't you remember? You told me to come anyway, that I didn't have to make things right first—that he would do that after I came."

I'm glad God delights to make things right, to cover our shame so we can stop trying to cover it ourselves. One of my favorite places to remember this is in Psalm 22. Tradition has it that this psalm is a prophetic messianic cry. And here we see that Messiah covers us by taking our naked shame and letting us walk away clothed. That Jesus takes our shame is poignantly expressed: "But I am a worm and not a man, / scorned by men and despised by the people. / All who see me mock me; / they hurl insults, shaking their heads. / . . . I am poured out like water. / . . . My heart has turned to wax. / . . . People stare and gloat over me. / They . . . cast lots for my clothing" (Psalm 22:6-18).

When I was four years old I loved all this about Jesus, even though I hadn't heard this psalm. Sitting in the Catholic church with my mother, I kneeled, stood, fidgeted and sighed. I ignored the grown-up talk of the priests. But I was mesmerized by the giant crucifix hanging behind the altar. It didn't quite capture the shame of Psalm 22; the plaster Jesus in that church was pale and smooth and had a loincloth tucked neatly over his private parts, while many scholars agree that Jesus was probably naked on the cross. But still, the crown of thorns, the head bowed in sorrow; they drew me to him in admiration and awe long before I met him over a white bread sandwich.

Today I see what he did even more richly, as if in 3-D. I feel like I'm wearing a pair of green plastic glasses and Jesus' work as portrayed in Psalm 22 jumps out at me in every scene. If you've ever watched a 3-D movie, you understand how this three-dimensionality can make a person almost breathless.

In the heart of the psalm, where Jesus cries prophetically through David that he's a worm, my breathlessness becomes acute. I don't expect other people to feel this way, but I can't help gasping. The very week I dredged up memories for this chapter—resurrected the Christmas stocking incident that made me feel like an unveiled worm—a friend quoted Psalm 22. We talked about the Hebrew word for *worm*, and I came home to revisit the psalm. I felt as if God were giving me an intimate gift.

The worm, of course, is a symbol of shame. It shows up in other Scriptures too, as when Job laments, "God has made me a byword to everyone, / a man in whose face people spit. / . . . If I say . . . to the worm, 'My mother' or 'My sister,' / where then is my hope?" (Job 17:6, 14). Jesus, unlike Job, goes all the way. He doesn't just consider calling the worm "Mother" or "Sister"; he becomes the worm itself. He takes on the full form of shame, saying, "I am a worm and not a man."

And now I can't help but do what Judith Kunst notes the rabbis do with the Scriptures—turn them and turn them again in a reverent, holy play. If I turn this passage, I see that the worm in Psalm 22 can be far more than a symbol for shame. After all, the Hebrew word here, *towla*, refers to a special sort of worm—a female that attaches herself to a tree before laying her eggs. Once she lays her eggs, this sacrificial mother becomes a protective covering. She dies right there, excreting a crimson fluid that covers both her body and her offspring.

Such colorful artistry was not lost on the ancients. They gathered this scarlet creature and crushed her to produce a crimson dye. And crimson, right up there with blue and purple, was used to dye wildly expensive clothing and tapestries. So it seems that Jesus, crushed in shame, offers to cover my nakedness—not only with the linen of his life, but also with an exotic color reserved for the rich and royal.

Just picturing this wine-crimson grace, I feel my soul tingle, as if it's growing wings. And the shame of my past, though real, cannot keep me earthbound.

3

tossed treasure ~ messiness

Spring picks at the snowdrifts week by week until they melt away. The air comes alive with gurgles and wood scent and, once again, my sister and I escape to the forest to play in the shadows for hours on end. Sometimes at a bend in the creek we laze on our favorite resting stone and plan our escape. We are growing, and we think we could walk far, far away. Yet always, when night falls, we emerge hungry, feet dragging. Tonight we trek back to the house only to fall to our knees in the front yard. My half-polished collection of tiny stones is scattered over crabgrass and pitted earth. Nearby, my toy rock tumbler sprawls, broken open, sand spit over its red plastic body. The short cord points upward as if to accuse heaven, but it's clear that my tumbler and its unfinished stones have traveled out the guest room window, from some human hand.

My stepfather was a messmaker. He tossed my treasures; he filled my life with scraps of betrayal. Sometimes his messes floated in broad daylight. Other times they sank to hidden places. The guest room, from which he tossed my rock tumbler, was one such hidden place. The door was often locked.

Behind that door my stepfather housed our newborn puppies. They messed on the floor while waiting to discover if he would keep them or drown them in the pond. I loved those puppies, litter after litter. But inevitably the small and weak ones were put in a burlap sack and tossed into the water. In the corner of that same guest room a jumble of furniture languished. It was the furniture my stepfather had shared with his mistress in their city apartment during a time when he returned to my mother only for pressed white shirts, venison with mashed potatoes or the curve of her flannel nightgown. Just thinking about that room and its messes makes me sick inside.

Sometimes I muse about why my stepfather was so good at making messes. I wonder if his talent sprang from a childhood during which he was at times undisciplined, at others beaten soundly. Or perhaps his messy tendencies grew from his nightmarish memories of World War II, of men crucified naked and upside down on Mussolini's scaffolds (he showed us pictures once and choked back tears). Or maybe his ragged ways were the influence of a stony heart untouched by God's transforming hands. But I will never be sure. My stepfather was a closed book scribbled with forbidding hatred.

As a child living with such an inscrutable messmaker, I often drifted into wishful daydreaming. I liked to think about a character in one of my Dr. Seuss books: the Cat in the Hat. This cat was no ordinary cat. He had peppermint candy stripes on his top hat, could walk on his long hind legs and talked with the finesse of a modern politician. He balanced a fish and a dish, a cake and a rake, and a little toy man in a tiny toy ship—all while bouncing on a striped rubber ball and fanning his juvenile spectators with a trendy red tail fan.

Even more impressive, when gravity had its way and what went up came down, he assured his young spectators, "Have no fear of this mess." And they had no reason to tremble because he rode back into the house with a marvelous, multi-armed mess-eating machine. Then he set the whole place in order before Mother came home.

In my childish fantasies, I sometimes wished for a personal Cat in the Hat with his handy mess-eating machine. God knows there was much to set in order in our home.

Now that I'm an adult, this fantasy persists in some form. I wish I could invite the Cat in the Hat into the messy places on this earth. If he was too busy entertaining toddlers, I'd be satisfied to obtain one of those lean, mean cleaning machines for myself—world-sized with rechargeable batteries.

Alas, the truth is, we all have to live with some pretty deep litter. Because even if we clean up our lives by coming to Christ, there are plenty of messmakers ready to toss our half-polished stones out of windows and clutter our guest rooms with furniture of questionable taste. Truly, a new life in Christ doesn't exempt us from messiness. Rather it can help us "accept the things we cannot change" and move forward.

As a child trapped in the messiness of a difficult household, I couldn't always accept things and move forward. There was plenty of anger and paralysis on my part, for I had a childlike perspective. I poured out my prayers like magic potions, expecting immediate results; when I did not get them, I doubted my God and lapsed into long periods of despair.

Today I understand things differently, particularly because of a picture that came to mind a few years ago when I was praying with my sister. She was going through a very tough family situation. Over and over we pleaded with God for mercy, for results. Why wouldn't he answer us? Didn't he care? These questions pecked at our faith. Then one night the picture flashed into my mind—a tangle of necklaces and patient fingers working at the links and knots, weaving up and down, in and out, steadily, lovingly.

I shared the image with my sister, and we reminisced about how our mother used to untangle the chains we pushed into her hands. But it took time. If we lost trust in her and pulled at the knots, they tightened. The message seemed clear. Yes God cared about my sister's situation. Yes he was working. And it was time for us to trust that he was acting in line with his grace. We needed to move forward in hope, even while we waited.

One of my favorite examples of a person who braved the waiting times is the biblical figure Priscilla. This woman suffered at the hands of a major messmaker, yet she managed to glide through the rubble with grace, dignity and a generous spirit.

To consider what she suffered, I imagine I am a modern Priscilla. A policeman knocks at my door. It is barely dawn; he knows he'll find me unprepared. Before I can process what's happening, he handcuffs me to my family, drags me out of my house and marches me through the streets to the train station. Lights flick on in my neighbors' houses as I pass. They will help me. Surely they see which direction we are walking.

A few hours later at the station, I'm relieved to see the faces of my neighbors as well as many other morning commuters. Now someone will speak on my family's behalf and on behalf of others in my community who've been marched here. My daughter is crying but I cannot reach my pocket to hand her a tissue. I'm relieved when one of my neighbors steps forward.

Relief melts to shock when my neighbor brushes by, and I see that she is wearing a scarf my friend brought me from China. She shields her face from the sun, and I note that my grandmother's pearl ring is on her finger. Someone has provided a microphone on the station platform, and my neighbor takes it to speak to the crowd. What follows I can't begin to describe. She greets us with a string of obscenities and accusations and tells us to go find another community to mess up. Neighbor after neighbor steps forward to do the same.

Finally a train pulls into the station, but neither my neighbors nor the commuters get on. "Reserved for Christian troublers," a sign in the window reads. The police uncuff us and push us onto the cars. We ride all day and night until we are tossed from the train three states away. A rumpled tissue I've finally given to my daughter is not enough to contain her tears.

In essence, this is the kind of thing that happened to Priscilla, a former Rome-dweller. The Bible speaks flatly about Priscilla's presence in Corinth, assuming that the hearers knew the situation: "Claudius had ordered all the Jews to leave Rome" (Acts 18:2). This hardly begins to express what happened.

Claudius's edict was swift and cruel. The Jews were subjected to degradation in the public square. One day they had homes and belongings; the next day they were victims of sanctioned property theft. They were forced to relocate from their communities. Claudius ordered this messmaking because, he claimed, the Jews were troublemakers who didn't deserve the right to live in Rome.

I marvel that despite this painful and humiliating mess, Priscilla went on to be a gracious and hospitable woman. She moved forward in hope while she waited to feel God's hand at work.

We know, for instance, that she and her husband sheltered the apostle Paul and even risked their necks for him (Acts 18:2; Romans 16:4). I find this remarkable considering how much Priscilla and Aquila had already lost. My own response to a barrage of messiness is often to hunker down in self-protection—not to open myself to more exposure and pain.

Furthermore, my self-protection can sometimes take the shape of verbal barbs or inflexibility. In this Priscilla and Aquila challenge me too. After only a year and a half in their new Corinthian surroundings, they agreed to uproot and sail with Paul to Syria to share the good news of Jesus. And we find that Priscilla and Aquila invited the teacher Apollos into their home, where they graciously corrected him (Acts 18:18, 24-26).

The textual placement of Priscilla's name before Aquila's in this particular story suggests she may have taken the lead in their gracious correcting. If this is so, then she beautifully embodies the Proverbs 31 woman: "She opens her mouth with wisdom, / and the teaching of kindness is on her tongue" (Proverbs 31:26 NRSV).

It is almost certain that Priscilla had other Proverbs 31 qualities as well, such as being "clothed with strength and dignity; / she can laugh at the days to come" (Proverbs 31:25). Of the seven times

Priscilla is mentioned in Scripture, six place her name before her husband's: Priscilla (or Prisca) and Aquila. Scholars observe that this was highly unusual in ancient public documentation, and they conclude that Priscilla probably made a huge impression on the early church. I consider that if she had protractedly mourned Claudius's mess or questioned God's grace again and again, she'd never have made such an impact.

Sometimes I wonder what helped Priscilla grow into such a gracious person, and my theories revolve around tents. Tents, after all, were central to her life.

She was first and foremost a tentmaker. As a maker of transient housing, Priscilla had opportunity to reflect on the transience of life. She may have, in quiet moments of binding leather to leather, found reason to decide that life really was as Paul said: "light and momentary troubles . . . achieving for us an eternal glory that far outweighs them all" (2 Corinthians 4:17). And how intimately she would have understood Paul's hopeful reminder: "If the earthly tent we live in is destroyed, we have a building from God" (2 Corinthians 5:1). Such realizations would have prepared her to face the mess of unfair change with a wisdom and hope that sees past present circumstances.

If tentmaking was not a door to this kind of hope, perhaps memories from her Jewish past were. As a child Priscilla would have celebrated with her family in a tentlike dwelling during Sukkot. Sukkot is a Jewish festival that remembers the Hebrews' survival in the Sinai wilderness. At its heart is the realization that life is impermanent and that we cannot find complete security in this messy world.

During Sukkot the family crowds together in a tent of sorts to share abundant food and community. It's an ironic festival, pairing abundance and communal security with remembrance of insecurity. In line with its paradoxical nature, the festival has two additional names: "time of our joy" and "festival of the ingathering." Perhaps it was in the Sukkah (tent) that Priscilla first learned an important lesson: Where the messmakers leave us empty and insecure, God can fill our hearts with hope, joy and a sense of gracious generosity.

At minimum, Priscilla knew she worshiped a Messiah who had "pitched his tent among us." This is the original language of John 1:14, which Jesus expanded when he told his followers, "Foxes have holes and birds of the air have nests, but the Son of Man has no place to lay his head" (Matthew 8:20). In other words, Jesus himself had left the predictability of heaven to camp down here and die at the hands of messmakers. Maybe Priscilla decided that if Jesus could make his bed on the ground and maintain a spirit of gracious hospitality, she could too.

After all these years as a Christian, it's still sometimes hard for me to relate to Priscilla's gracious, courageous posture in the face of messiness. Furthermore, I don't know much about tents the way she did. I live in a tiny Tudor made of solid stucco. I avoid sleeping less than two feet from the ground. I don't like makeshift dwellings or cold floors. Honestly, I like predictability, comfort and security. I think I always have.

In quiet childhood moments, especially during those long periods of despair when I couldn't see God's hands at work, I did consider the choices of certain friends. Some planned elaborate escapes by turning to suicidal razors, car exhaust or strong drink. Unable to secure a mess-eating Cat in the Hat machine, they took matters into their own hands. Maybe I would have done so, too, if I hadn't tumbled into the creekbed to rest on a moss-licked stone.

4

HERON ROAD ~ SUFFERING

In the heat of summer we take to the road that drifts from our house toward pines and wild strawberries. We seek the shade of towering firs, laugh out loud, hold our mother's hands. Occasionally we see the blue heron in the middle of our path. Sometimes he stands serene and silent, waiting for God knows what . . . a certain slant of light, a cloud to pass, the call of a swamp frog. Then he disappears to heaven with a massive shuddering, his giant wings casting a crosslike shadow on the oiled dirt and shale. Today the heron does not appear, but my sister and I walk with our mother over his usual path.

It is time, we say, to take this road in one direction. No turning back. If you want to stay, we understand, but we've arranged a passage for ourselves: our real father's door is open. We watch her cheeks blush and glisten, her hands play at the edges of her shirt. This is, to us, the quivering moment when wings start beating and air starts flowing and the shadow begins to fall away. Will she stay here, breathing smoke and threat and sorrow, or will she join our flight? Field insects sing. Dust rises and falls in the setting sun. The strawberries ripen, burst with fruity scent. At last, we sigh with the relief of years when she takes our hands and walks.

When I consider my mother and her decision to marry my step-father, I remember a story about Salvador Dali. As a budding artist he painted with stones, attaching tiny rocks to his canvas. He glued cherry stems to a still life. His parents supported his creative efforts and hung his stone sky painting in the dining room. Every once in a while a pebble would dive to the floor with a tap. Salvador's father assured people, "It's nothing; it's just another stone that has dropped from our child's sky." Then he added, "The ideas are good, but who would ever buy a painting that would eventually disappear while the house grew cluttered with stones?"

It seems my mother had a vision as naively hopeful as Salvador's when she married my stepfather. Her marriage to my own father had ended abruptly when he took a mistress just three years into their marriage. With my father gone, she picked up stones and started painting—an older man with strength and charm, a knee to bounce her children, a wedding ring to shine. These stones were a poor medium, though possibly better than cherry stems. She would regret this choice night after night for years on end as the stones gradually jumped from her painting like little kamikazes, leaving a blank sky and a floor littered with sharp objects.

I don't understand what kept my mother standing before that picture for so long. Perhaps the very things that had first caused her to pick up stones and paint: fear and loneliness, or even hope. Perhaps she did it for us, her children. Yes, we were cutting our feet with every step, but we had a house (when he didn't lock the doors and nail the windows shut), and a car (when he didn't hide the keys), and food (when he didn't throw it into the snow). This was a promotion from her childhood experience, when she and her siblings hid beneath the buffet and watched their father grind steel-toed boots into their mother's face.

Fortunately, my sister and I knew nothing about our mother's difficult childhood at the time we took her for The Walk to say we'd had enough of my stepfather. Maybe we would have faltered if we'd known—maybe caved to the thought that our situation was bad but not the worst, so why leave? Thus, in our fortunate ignorance, we two young teenagers put it to her: leave our stepfather or we leave you.

I believe that many quiet conversions to Christianity happen like this. People look at their feet and realize they are cut and bruised, so they reach out for the balm of Gilead (Jeremiah 8:22). In fortunate ignorance, they leave their old life behind without thinking, *Well, I'm okay—at least I still have my feet. That God stuff is only for people who are missing toes and arches and can no longer walk without support.*

I know people like this—the quiet-conversion types—but I also know people who didn't look to heaven until they were lying on the ground. According to God, this is the difference between ford-ing the gentle waters of Shiloah and slamming from rock to rock in the mighty flood of Assyria. We can gather this from the case of ancient Israel, God's beloved. She would not be wooed with God's gentle leadings, which he compared to the calm waters of Shiloah, so he gave her over to the Assyrians. These invaders became a "rock one stumbles over," and many Israelites fell and were broken before they turned to God for rescue (Isaiah 8:5-7, 14-15).

When trying to get our attention, God prefers Shiloah, hands down. But he will do what it takes to lead us to him, even if it means bringing on Assyria. This is a little scary, to say the least. Ancient Assyria was over the top. They did things like adorn their city walls with human heads.

Frankly, I've doubted God's taste in using the Assyrias of our lives to birth something new. Not only is it unfashionable, it's also harrowing and bloody. I puzzle over it, thinking, *how can he do it— allow and even assist us into the hard tunnel of suffering? How can he go around knocking rocks off our sky paintings with a sledgehammer? Why would he make us walk on the stone-cluttered floor?*

As Moses said to the Israelites, sometimes God humbles us by letting us hunger so we learn that he is the only true bread (Deuteronomy 8:3). Moses or not, I'm uncomfortable with this technique, and I've shared my opinion with God. It doesn't seem to bother him; he just gives me more reading material—like the prophet Isaiah and a common Gospel parable.

In Isaiah we hear a song about a vineyard, which I think was based on a top-ten hit of the time. It starts out normally enough. If we close our eyes we can picture the scene—Isaiah standing in the public square singing with his politician's voice, people mildly amused but starting to hum along. Then as the words take a turn, we see frowns; a few protective parents cover their children's ears and the crowd dissipates. Isaiah strikes the last note standing eye to eye with a donkey, who mindlessly flicks a fly off his leg and blinks.

Perhaps this is not precisely how it went, but the point is that Isaiah was not popular at that moment. And who could blame his listeners? Isaiah sang that when Assyria came to Israel, the Israelites would be dying of hunger and parched with thirst, that their root would become rotten and their blossoms blow away like dust. He even sang that their corpses would be like garbage in the streets (Isaiah 5:13, 24-25). Sometimes I try to imagine what would happen if our president sang a song like this on ABC's *Primetime*. Isaiah, however, seemed remarkably ignorant of the polls. His message was honest to a fault.

The most disturbing part of Isaiah's message is God's own words. The Almighty says he will stretch out his hand against his people and strike them. He will make his people a waste and tell the rain not to fall on them. He will call a nation from far away to tear the Israelites limb from limb, as a lion would (Isaiah 5:29). If God lived on my street and said this to his children, someone would probably call protective services. Maybe it would even be me.

Yet protection is ultimately God's goal, even if his safety net looks more like a string of landmines. This is hard to put in perspective. After all, God is a God of love. The idea that he'd let us become a bruised reed just to reveal that we should reach out to him . . . this seems harsh, but something Jesus said can help us understand.

Jesus told his disciples that they shouldn't fear what can happen to the body; they should only fear what can happen to the soul (Matthew 10:28). This suggests that God's Assyria method, though exceedingly hard and painful, has merit—as a way to save the soul and keep it from a worse fate. Of course, God prefers that we come to him on the gentle waters of Shiloah. It's not like he wants us to suffer. But if we scorn Shiloah, we may discover that we've asked for Assyria.

In his book *The Return of the Prodigal Son*, Henri Nouwen examines a famous painting by Rembrandt and uses it to weave a moving portrait of someone who chose Assyria by refusing Shiloah. It is, of course, the prodigal son. Most people will remember the story as Jesus told it. A younger son goes to his father and requests an early inheritance—which, Nouwen notes, is like saying, "I wish you were dead." Despite the deeply insulting nature of the request, the father gives him his share and the son leaves for a distant country, eventually squandering everything. He ends up sleeping with pigs and wishing he could eat their slop.

This is a turning point. The prodigal says to himself, "How many of my father's hired hands have bread enough and to spare, but here I am *dying of hunger!*" (Luke 15:17 NRSV, emhasis mine). In these words I hear Moses and Isaiah. Moses: he humbled you by *letting you hunger.* Isaiah: my people are *dying of hunger.* And this is a turning point for me. I see, suddenly, that God's Assyria method is something we choose. We hunger not because he wants to starve us but because we've declined to eat at his table. God's words in Isaiah echo here: "It is you who have ruined my vineyard" (Isaiah 3:14).

Nouwen observes this truth in Rembrandt's painting. Examining the son's image, he says, "The soles of [the prodigal's] feet tell the story of a long and humiliating journey. The left foot, slipped out of its worn sandal, is scarred. The right foot, only partially covered by a broken sandal, also speaks of suffering and misery." As if unable to walk further without support, the prodigal is depicted on his knees, leaning into the father's robes. His suffering cripples him to the ground. It is etched into his feet by sharp stones that must have cluttered his path.

Gazing at this picture of suffering, I realize it was the prodigal, not his father, who chose that path, those stones, and walked to a distant country. And it deepens my thinking about the process. What looks to us like God smashing rocks off our painting is actually the natural outcome of our chosen medium. If we paint with stones, gravity will pull them into our path—sometimes violently so.

Turning back to Isaiah's vineyard song, we hear the prophet humming that the Israelites have gone wild and God has said, so be it. You want to be wild grapes? Then I'll remove your hedge and break down your wall. You may grow where you wish, even in the desert, even in Assyria (Isaiah 5:5). But always remember, I'll be waiting for you when you come home. In fact, I'll abandon my pride and run to meet you when you hobble back—as if I'm the child greeting the old, tired man (Luke 15:20).

This is the side of God I know and love, the side I always suspect even when it looks like he's being unfair. And knowing the depth of his love, the childish delight he takes in us, it's difficult for me to understand why some choose a hard, wayward journey to him. But in the end, the nature of our journey is largely unimportant. Shiloah, Assyria, downtown New York—never mind, as long as our path leads us to the arms of God. When I consider that my sister and I took such different paths, for instance, all that matters to me is that we are now walking in the same grace, holding each other's hands.

What grieves and perplexes me most is the person who, when faced with Assyria and the slop trough, goes down screaming and never takes God's gracious hand or rises from his knees. As Proverbs 19:3 explains, there are some who, after their folly leads to ruin, rage in their hearts against the Lord. This can be dangerous for the people in close proximity. A man who stays to face his death in Assyria may decide he wants company—someone else's head next to his on the city wall. In this, I grieve for my stepfather. He chose Assyria and tried to keep us at his side.

5

SWORD IN THE STONE ~ RESISTANCE

I am no longer in my stepfather's house, and it is bittersweet—bitter to say goodbye to the creek and the forest and the midnight walks where moonlight bathed the fields in silver—yet sweet to be free . . . if this can be called freedom. My stepfather, hunter that he is, has begun to track me. I know that his war-torn fingers are trained to ease a trigger, and I remember how he fed us fawns, and mothers and fathers of fawns, throughout the years. I cannot forget the sinews in my plate, or the carcasses falling limp from the back of a blue pickup, or the white bellies hung on an old maple tree. My stepfather's recent phone calls to my mother are the paralyzing beams of a hunter's headlights; I do not doubt that he will do as he is promising. Take aim and fire.

As soon as my mother left my stepfather, he began to threaten our lives. Thinking back, I cringe for my mother. I'm a parent myself now, and I consider the options she had before her. Should she tell us my stepfather's plans? Or should she guard our hearts?

Most parents prefer to guard their children's hearts. I know I do.

In this way, I am much like a writer I once heard at our local library. When she read from her book *Why Animals Sleep So Close to the Road, and Other Lies I Tell My Children*, I could relate to her desire to protect her two-year-old from the wiles of Disney. "Disney has a formula," she said, referring to the movie company's habit of killing off fathers and mothers on-screen. "And I have a formula for Disney," she quipped. She told her children, "Bambi's mother didn't really die. They'll meet up in a sequel."

This is a fine approach in some circumstances. After all, I have a psychologist friend who says it's not good to frighten children unduly; they need to approach life with confidence. On the other hand, I think Bambi's mother would have lobbied for the straightforward approach: tell the hard truth, especially when life is at stake. I suspect this because she forthrightly told her toddler fawn, "Don't run into the open. Man is in the forest."

My mother chose this tell-it-like-it-is approach. Our stepfather was enraged by our departure. He'd begun to call and describe in graphic detail what he planned to do, so she warned her two young teens, "Man is in the forest."

Fortunately, the people from my little church knew what to do. They knew that an order of protection wouldn't stop a man who planned to shoot himself after setting his sights on us. So they came to pray in our new apartment.

I still remember the circle of their arms, how their prayers poured into the room. At the time it seemed they came to do the impossible—to pull a sword from a stone, to show who had the true power in a dark and hopeless time. Really, they saw the situation in its fullness. This was not simply about a man gone crazy. It was about an unseen battle raging in the heavens. So they approached the problem with spiritual resistance, with prayer.

For weeks after those people encircled us with their spirit-filled prayers, I walked on eggshells. Some days at school I broke down in the middle of classes or hid in the bathroom crying. I could not explain my fears to friends; they were concerned with physics tests and basketball scores and who was going to the prom with whom. All of that seemed frivolous in comparison to my fear of being found and cornered.

As the weeks wore on, however, my fear drifted and finally dissipated. The spiritual approach to our earthly problem proved to be wise and effective. After the church people prayed, my stepfather retreated. I never saw his face or heard his voice again.

Reflecting on this, it seems to me that those praying people must have read the book of Daniel. Because in Daniel we learn that our earthly lives intersect with unseen spiritual forces. The godly messenger who visits Daniel explains, "Since the first day that you set your mind to gain understanding . . . your words were heard, and I have come in response to them" (Daniel 10:12).

But a perplexing question arises—if Daniel's words were heard from the beginning, why did it take twenty-one days for this messenger to arrive? Apparently, the prince of Persia, an evil angel, had opposed the messenger for twenty-one days, so he enlisted Michael, "one of the chief princes," to take over so he could leave the heavenly battle scene and come to Daniel (Daniel 10:13).

Now if God's own messengers have to bother with spiritual battles, it's unlikely that we can go bobbing into every open glen without considering the stalking Enemy. In fact, 1 Peter 5:8 cautions us that Satan is like a roaring lion, looking for unsuspecting whitetails to devour. This puts a damper on free frolic in the forest, but it needn't paralyze us.

On this note, I like to remember Martin Luther's attitude. In *What Has Christianity Ever Done for Us?* Jonathan Hill says Luther "regarded [the devil] with contempt rather than fear. When he heard the devil stomping around at night, he would mutter, 'Oh, it's just you,' and go back to sleep." Luther resisted the devil by refusing to even pay attention to him. In this way, Luther did not let Satan interfere with his work, and he translated the New Testament for his fellow Germans in eleven weeks' time.

Unfortunately, some of us lose precious time, effectiveness, charity and even reputation because we refuse to pay attention to the devil in an altogether different way than Luther. We live in blissful ignorance of the devil's crossbow because we hesitate to believe he's real. Or if we believe he's real, we neglect to put on our armor.

I understand both these tendencies because I live with them in my own mind and heart. First of all, as a "prove it to me" person, I find it difficult to picture the invisible evil that stalks us. I'm used to thinking in terms of the visible—in terms of real things. It's not natural for me to think about what I can't see, to point to the empty air and say, "Something is there."

To correct my tendency to ignore the invisible, I turn to science. I remember that scientists affirm invisible causes in the face of a visible effect. The tides ebb and flow; scientists credit invisible gravity. The atom holds together; they assert the power of invisible electrical attraction. So I translate this way of thinking to my faith: a Christian falters . . . perhaps a fiery, invisible dart has lodged in the soul unnoticed.

I also consider history, remembering that strategic enemies don't announce their arrival. Ancient Persia's triumph over Babylon is a prime example. The Persians got a clever idea: divert the river leading under Babylon's walls, then march in undetected on dry ground to claim a glorious and powerful kingdom. Again, I apply this to my faith. If the sneaky red halfling with the pointy tail really exists in some less ridiculous form, would he want me to believe it? Not if he were smart. Rather, I think he'd want me to keep the party rolling unawares, like the king of Babylon. Then he could redirect the water that feeds my soul. I wouldn't even notice him tiptoe into my mind and heart on dry ground.

Yet more than through science and more than through history, I've come to hear the rustle of the Evil One through the experience of a dear friend. This person is peaceful and levelheaded. But she wasn't always so; there was a time when she actively consorted with demons. The spirits were very nice to her and treated her like a special friend. They didn't question her fantasies of being an enviro-terrorist. Nor were they bothered by her plan to engage in sacrificial suicide.

But when she developed an earthly love relationship, they turned nasty and threatening. The only solution she found was to act on a suggestion in a witchcraft book. "If spirits bother you too much," it said, "focus on the light that is Jesus." The suggestion worked and today she's a free woman. For me, this has been like meeting the demon-delivered Mary in person. The testimony of a freed, visible woman increases my consciousness of the invisible hunter.

Yet even with an increased awareness that the devil exists, I'm too often unprepared to meet his invisible presence. I need reminders to act as Paul recommended. "Put on the full armor of God," he said, "so that you can take your stand against the devil's schemes. . . . And pray in the Spirit on all occasions" (Ephesians 6:11, 18).

Paul is serious about this advice. Speaking urgently, he says, "For our struggle is not against flesh and blood, but against the rulers, against the authorities, against the powers of this dark world and against the spiritual forces of evil in the heavenly realms" (Ephesians 6:12). From Paul's perspective there's an invisible hunting party on our heels, complete with decoys, bloodhounds and automatic rifles.

But we can advance confidently through the forest nonetheless. Because the whole armor of God covers us head to toe. It includes the belt of truth, the breastplate of righteousness, the shoes of gospel proclamation, the shield of faith, the helmet of salvation, the sword of the Spirit and the power of prayer.

I admit that sometimes I leave this armor in its case just when I should be putting it on in earnest. Perhaps this seems surprising since I faced a flesh-and-blood hunter long ago. But I falter. Sometimes it's a matter of pride. Or I'm frail and forgetful. Other times I'm lazy or embarrassed. I also have a learned distaste for war that makes me reticent, despite the need to stand prepared for a battle that burns whether or not I want it to.

Because the battle is hard and I'm sometimes unprepared, I take comfort in our gracious Jesus. He prays for me and leads me through the woods, and by his Spirit he warns me, "Watch out. The Evil One is in the forest."

6

HOWE'S CAVE ~ BAPTISM

Living in an apartment with my mother and sister, I rarely go anywhere any-more. My mother's sixty-hour workweek eats her time, whisks her away until night falls. A highway hems us in at the front of our building; a fence blocks our way to flowering fields and mountains at the back. So it is refreshing to have an unexpected visit from my grandmother. Today she's come to take me to a nearby attraction: Howe's Cave. After she pays for our entrance, she wraps gnarled fingers around my hand and pulls me into the iron-barred elevator.

We descend. How many feet into the jagged earth? The guide tells us, mono-tone, but I forget in favor of more pressing details, like clammy air pushing into my lungs and darkness that is barely countered by dusty bulbs. I lean into Grandma's voluminous bosom until we come to a stop and exit to a silent world of stalactite and stalagmite—forbidding swords of some dragon's lair that hang and rise.

I'm fairly confident I'd never make a good spelunker. Spelunkers explore caves with a lamp attached to their foreheads, as if that light could drive away such suffocating darkness. To me, any activity performed in full sun, even weeding a stubborn and unruly garden, is preferable.

My aversion to darkness and love of the light is helpful when I consider the continuing process of my faith—which is the movement of my soul from darkness to light. For many Christians, this movement is publicly signaled with a baptism, an outward ritual that marks association with Christ, of whom it is said, "What has come into being in him was life, and the life was the light of all people" (John 1:3-4 NRSV). In this way, baptism is an outward sign of an inward process: the soul, having been resuscitated to life by Christ, moves ever more clearly into light.

I only wish I'd been awake to the deeper, richer sense of baptism's symbols on the day I stepped into tepid water, closed my eyes to chlorine and a pastor. But as Lauren Winner notes, sometimes we, like the Israelites, have to use that little phrase out of Exodus 24, *Na'aseh v'nishma:* We will do and we will understand. Sometimes the doing brings the understanding. Sometimes, as in my case, there's an embarrassing time gap between the act and the illumination.

I got baptized as a teenager. Again. This, of course, makes me a double-dipper. The first dip had been unconscious; my mother took me, sleeping, to the priest. The second dip, the one I got as a teenager, was conscious, but I may as well have been a sleeping baby for all I understood about baptism.

It wasn't my understanding of the ritual that drew me to this second baptism; it was the invitation of my history teacher and his wife. We'd started going to the same evangelical church, which happened to be running a special offer on baptisms. My teacher noted that he and his wife were going to take the offer, and he asked me to consider doing so too. In the end I decided to join them. It was a bit like going along to McDonald's for ketchup and fries. Buy two get one free. It seemed like the thing to do at the time.

After a few baptism classes we went to the recesses of an old brick sanctuary I'd never seen before. To my great surprise, a few men lifted a section of floor to reveal a secret swimming pool. I had brief visions of congregants sneaking in for a midnight dip, but the pool was small and shallow, and it didn't even have a diving board.

I don't remember much about the baptism itself. Mostly I remember the important things. Like my teacher's wife in her bathing suit—back bent, belly swollen like Sylvia Plath's melon on tendrils. And my teacher's face, Cro-Magnon, rising from the baptismal—water riding down the curl of his lashes, dripping from his broad nose.

I don't even remember stepping into the pool. Don't know what I wore. What faces, if any, looked on. What prayers (surely there were some) or words echoed in that place. It was like being at a sad pool, the blue fluorescent lights peering down, wondering, why are these people here? What does it all mean? If I had it to do over again, it would be different—if I knew then what I know now.

When I think of baptism now, I think of a kaleidoscope. See here, the world is crimson snowflakes. Look again, it's purple stars. Held to a brighter light, everything turns in crystalline brilliance. It takes more than one turn to explain what John the Baptist inaugurated at the Jordan River, to reveal the richness of what we enact today when we descend into the water.

Though water is mostly a symbol of life in the Bible, it also holds its terrors. The psalmist strummed and sang, "The cords of death entangled me; the / torrents of destruction overwhelmed me" (Psalm 18:4). Water is bottomless, consuming. I think of that last scene in Jane Campion's film *The Piano*, when the protagonist purposely inserts her foot into the rope coil attached to her piano. Soon after, her husband heaves the instrument overboard and she descends into the depths, face frozen in rippled sorrow. Water is death, not only life.

Job tells me that water is also home to Leviathan, a "monster in the waters" (Job 3:8; Psalm 74:13). Moses reminds me it is chaos (Genesis 1:2). And I shiver with Jonah as he recalls,

The engulfing waters threatened me,
> the deep surrounded me;
> seaweed was wrapped around my head.

To the roots of the mountains I sank down;
> the earth beneath barred me in forever.
> (Jonah 2:5-6)

In light of everything that water meant to these ancients, descending into its depths during baptism is like opening a door—inviting curious onlookers to peer into the chaos, hear the beating of a dragon heart, lament how the soul seems crushed by weight of darkness. In the same instant it's an invitation to expectation. A rescue is being played out. A creation is being enacted. The one who descends celebrates ascension to a re-created life that teems with lilies and peaches, eagles and red-eyed tree frogs.

I wish I'd thought about all this when I decided to go along with my teacher and his wife. I might have invited my friends, told a few people what we were about to do, treated it less like ketchup and fries.

I think the people of Jesus' time understood better. They had a tradition. If a Gentile wanted to convert to Judaism, he engaged in a once-for-all ritual washing—a mikvah. Naked, the convert descended into a pool of living water. This immersion was counted null if even the width of a bean string accidentally prevented water from touching the space between two teeth. (They must have had a pretty thorough saturation examination afterward to check for this sort of thing.) The mikvah signaled a totally new life, which is why it was said that any Gentile who was submerged had completely separated from his past. He was considered to be like a newborn child.

A newborn travels from darkness to light, from water to warm, dry arms. And from breathlessness to wide swallows of air. He journeys into life and can never turn back. Maybe this is why the early Christians chose the name *baptism* to describe what John initiated at the Jordan. The term was associated with a no-turning-back process—dyeing cloth. Once dipped, always stained. I can't help but think again of Psalm 22, where David prophetically compares Messiah to a worm crushed for crimson dye.

This kind of indelible change was already associated with the Jordan in the minds of the Hebrew people. For, long before Jesus came, the Israelites crossed the Jordan from east to west, from crust to milk and honey, from life as wanderers to life settled down (see Joshua 4). The Jordan had also been a backdrop for Elijah's fiery ascension to heaven. It reflected his whirlwind journey from life to eternal life (2 Kings 2:6-12).

So the Jordan was a culturally and historically rich place to stage the first baptisms. How far from the dank, bleached pool I was baptized in. How grand and public in declaring God's search and rescue compared to the back room of an old brick sanctuary.

Knowing this, if I were to be baptized today, I would search out a popular river in lieu of a church baptismal. Perhaps I'd poke into the riverbed and collect twelve stones to take home for my garden—as the Israelites chose twelve stones from the center of the bounded Jordan, to set up so they would remember to fear God and so the whole earth would recognize his mighty hand (Joshua 4:24). Or maybe I would celebrate a Passover ceremony as they did soon after crossing, remembering how the destroyer had breathed at doorpost and lintel but had turned away. I might also welcome the chance, on ascending, to sip a creamy glass of milk and honey—milk, the drink of a newborn child and a biblical symbol of life.

I wish I'd thought of these things when I plunged into that tired old pool. I wish, too, that I could have emerged from the water into a constant sense of light and life. But the Christian experience isn't so simple, as some make it out to be. Indeed, it's more like what we see in Jacob's life. After he dunked in a roiling river, he ascended to a wrestling match that caused him all kinds of hip problems (see Genesis 32:22-31). He walked into a new future, but he did not do so without struggle and setback.

Struggle and setback. That's what awaited me as I packed my bags for college, leaving the banks of my baptism and my home behind. And even now, though grace has rescued me from the cave of my hidden past and heart, I'm sometimes assailed by struggle and setback. In moments when I least expect it.

7

paLisaDe cLiffs ~ DOUBt

Far away from my growing-up place where a country creek wound through my days and my dreams, I now live near a swift river that rolls past the Palisade Cliffs . . . sheer rocks that shine coppery in the sun, evidence of the passing of some ancient glacier. Across from these cliffs, an hour north of the big city, I'm at a small college tucked in the hills. I've come here to "grow my faith," but I feel that I'm about to drown.

So, today I'm talking to save my life, in a favorite professor's office. Words tumble, crush, bump into the stillness—strong accusations against the One who's given me life in so many ways. A seasoned face listens with concern, takes my heavy words and swallows them whole. A hand shows me the light of faith that burns even in this dark moment. A heart prays for this disciple who, like Peter, stepped out of the boat to meet Jesus only to doubt the moment and slip beneath the waves.

My former professor, David D., is an excellent customer service representative—you know the type: the attendant who goes beyond company script, who makes you feel you are a person with real needs and concerns. David will try to tell you otherwise, say that interpersonal relations are not his thing. But looking back, I find it serendipitous that he was the Christian on duty when I called the kingdom crisis hotline.

I don't remember what sparked the doubt that pushed me to the edge of faith and landed me in David's office. It could have been Philosophy 101. Or reading our perplexing Old Testament in detail for my college's Bible class. It could have been Marx or Skinner, or a natural exploration that came with leaving home for the first time. Maybe it was my sudden impression that a lot of the people at my Christian college had grown up safe and happy while I had grown up suffering violence and exposure.

In any case, something pushed me into crisis where I teetered on a dangerous cliff that could only drop into disbelief or rebellion. I began to question God's very existence. Even so, I talked to him: "If you exist, I don't want to know you. You send people to hell. You let people suffer. You think you're so great that everyone should worship you—how arrogant." I recall thinking I could not be a Christian anymore. I would not pretend at faith. It was time to walk away. I must have said something to this effect to David, and he invited me to come and talk, as many times as I wanted.

To this day, I'm thankful that when I showed up in his office over the months, he wrestled gently with my thoughts instead of trying to bind me into the kingdom with a clown smile on my face. He must have suspected my Jacob heart—the kind that sometimes risks injury to touch the truth. He must have understood my need to sort things out, and this didn't threaten him. He also must have known Jesus' famous words, "Blessed are those who have not seen and yet have believed" (John 20:29), but he did not draw the opposite conclusion: "Cursed are those who need to see." However, I'm confident he put me on his endangered disciples prayer list without delay, knowing what was at stake.

This was a wise move. After all, people in the "borderlands of belief," as Philip Yancey puts it, are vulnerable to attack. They are not prancing through the forest with the whole armor of God but have left the shield of faith in a shady glen and the belt of truth beside a fallen tree. This can be an honest, necessary course of action in the journey of faith, but things can happen in the meantime. Curses can overtake.

I remember what happened to King Saul in 1 Samuel 13 when he doubted in the midst of a battle. He had every reason to question God. People's lives were at stake and things were looking grim. The Israelites were facing a Philistine army of three thousand chariots, six thousand horsemen and troops like sand on the seashore. And Israel had six thousand men. To make matters worse, the prophet Samuel was late in coming to make the sacrifice to God. Shaken by doubt, Saul stood on the edge of faith.

One could say it was not doubt, but rather Saul's poor self-image and a deep desire to prove himself as Israel's new king that pushed him to the edge. In light of Saul's actions before this moment—how he hid and pretended and acted insecurely—this seems like an accurate assessment. However, I believe that the biblical writer who chronicled Saul's descent wanted to highlight doubt as the cause. We can infer this by listening to the writer's sly description of the enemy troops as "sand on the seashore." He could have used another comparison—salt in the sea, rocks on the mountain, olives in a harvest press. But he chose to talk sand.

Israel, of course, had a history of sand-talk from God. Sand meant a future. Abraham had been promised descendants more numerous than the sand on the shore, and from those descendants would come one who would save all the nations. But on Saul's battlefield, the promise suddenly seemed jeopardized. Israel was facing defeat before an army as numerous as sand on the seashore.

Suddenly the suspense in the narrative expands. Will Saul believe in God's age-old promise to Abraham enough to do the right thing and wait for the man of God to come and perform a holy sacrifice? Or will Saul doubt the promise? Unfortunately, he embraces doubt. So as his troops begin to sneak away, he offers a sacrifice to God before the prophet Samuel arrives.

I'm sure this seemed like the thing to do. I assume Saul offered the sacrifice to show his troops that he was in charge, to boost morale. But the act, conceived in doubt, cost him his kingdom. "You acted foolishly," Samuel explains. "You have not kept the command the LORD your God gave you; if you had, he would have established your kingdom over Israel for all time. But now your kingdom will not endure" (I Samuel 13:13-14).

Looking at Saul's tragedy, we discover that the dangers of doubt are real. We can get injured and suffer loss. The entire direction of our lives can change.

Yet the forces that fuel doubt are also real.

In his book *A Fragile Stone*, Michael Card examines the life of Peter. With poignant touch he describes Peter's moments of doubt. First, as Peter walks to Jesus on water, Card says, "something about the experiment went terribly wrong. . . . He began to sink. . . . In the very midst of the miracle he doubts the new reality he has just stepped into, and it all starts to unravel." Peter's life is suddenly, truly at risk. He feels the waves lapping at his toes. A fisherman by profession, he knows the sea is deep and cold. Maybe the water has even drowned someone he knew or loved. Perhaps real things nag him into doubt, as Card suggests.

Similarly, when Peter is faced with the reality that Jesus will die a criminal's death, doubt assails him. The truth is too difficult, too bloody, too dirty to hold. Jesus seems to be the vulnerable babe all over again. Can such a savior be king? Can he triumph to rule and reign? Many disciples shun the possibility and walk away, but Peter and the Twelve stay because there is "no place else to go." Again, Card makes a pointed observation. When we see Jesus in a new, unexpected way that fails to meet expectations, we are tempted to falter and say: This is hard; who can accept it?

A dangerous question indeed. When urged to the surface by real circumstances with real dangers, it may wrest us from the arms of God. Yet we must ask. For if the question is cornered and stifled, it can lead to another unexpected danger—eclipse of reason and departure from reasonable behavior.

I think this is why David D. cleared space in his office when I showed up saying, "This is hard; who can accept it?" I have to believe he understood that an unquestioned faith is questionable, that covering doubt and demanding unexamined allegiance holds its own special dangers.

I recently read a memoir called *Jesus Land*. It was graphic, and some people might be embarrassed to read it, yet I think it illustrates the point. The book was written by a woman who fell victim to Christian parents and a Christian reform school that preached, "Faith is blind," "What leaders do in Jesus' name is done with Jesus' approval," and "Never question."

The results were disastrous. Ordinary Christians justified everything from severe whippings to emotional neglect, racial bias to prisoner-of-war mind-control techniques. Needless to say, author Julia Scheeres, who swallowed abuse to save her skin, memorized Bible verses and gushed false praises to Jesus, does not have a bright view of Christianity. Her guides for life are "trust no one" and "subvert all rules." A constrictive faith caused her to question everything and write a book nudging others to do the same.

Perhaps Julia's life would have been different if she'd encountered the real Jesus—through parents, church and Christian schools. The real Jesus let Peter get out of the boat, knowing he would begin to sink in doubt. And the real Jesus waited for Peter to cry, "Save me!" before bearing him up. Might the real Jesus have let a doubting Peter drown if he hadn't cried out? I wonder.

Yet even as Jesus let Peter test the waters, he didn't abandon him, and so I believe it goes with us. When we test the waters, Jesus stands amidst the waves holding our gaze. Or he walks beside us on dangerous cliffs, extending a hand should we want to hold it. Ultimately he meets us on the ground, where, like Jacob who wrestled the angel, we can push and tackle him and plead for a blessing that will soak us to the bone.

In my professor's office I struggled like Jacob, on a hard cliff of doubt. In retrospect I see that this was good, despite its dangers. For my faith ultimately became stronger—and it would need to be to heal the past and usher in an unexpected future.

8

HOLDING pfaltzgraff ~ INCLUSION

I stay here near the river as my college days come to an end. Friends leave for distant places, but I love this water, these cliffs that glow in the evening sun. And I love coming home to my own place where I eat what I like on Pfaltzgraff dishes passed down to me from my mother. Each night I take this stoneware from the cabinet with my own hands, place my dinner on it and later push it into a sink of suds, wipe it clean. This simple, secret pleasure is born of years in my stepfather's house . . . years where my hands were idle because, he said, I was swine—too dirty to touch a dish or cut venison or spoon the mashed potatoes. Yes I relish being at this sink, holding Pfaltzgraff, while the crickets sing with abandon beneath a setting sun.

Most people are not enamored of household chores, especially washing the dishes. So I'm embarrassed to admit it, but I like to do dishes. I attribute this trait to my childlike attraction to water and suds, and a deep need to live on the inside. Doing dishes is a sign that I'm no longer the outsider I once was in my childhood home.

What a relief. Being on the outside is lonely. I know this first-hand, and I know this from looking at history.

I consider, for instance, the isolation of lepers in Europe from around A.D. 1100 to 1300. If it was discovered that a person had leprosy, life on the outside began in earnest. The sufferer was ushered into church, where a black tent stood like a cave at the altar. The leper was forced to kneel in the shadows of this tent while a priest intoned the burial mass. Then the leper journeyed outward to a leper house, where the priest threw a cascade of dirt at him, as if the leper were being lowered into his grave.

After this funereal sendoff, any foray into society was a grim reminder to the leper that he lived on the outside. He wore special clothes, was restricted from dipping in the local river, rang a bell to warn of his approach, spoke in a whisper (lest his breath caress another) and watched the children play without hope of ever holding them to his breast.

Some communities solved his problem with a simpler solution—they buried him alive.

This is an extreme example of the terror of being outside. Yet such experiences are still present at various times and places. In fact, I discovered in my young adulthood that I had the capacity to pitch a proverbial tent at the altar and push someone into it. I had, after all, learned that "difference" was dangerous. My stepfather had delighted to curse and call me person-of-color names. My paternal grandmother had extolled the promotion of birth control among less-than-desirable populations—anyone with dark skin or low intelligence.

So I grew up learning to listen for the sound of "difference" bells—the ring of which would raise an inexplicable fear in my heart and set my mind to silent name calling. Like my stepfather and my grandmother, I didn't see the impact this kind of attitude could have. After all, raising a tent in my hidden heart was not a real act, and I certainly had a diverse set of friends. So how much harm could my secret fears and thoughts cause?

A lot, apparently. I like how Susan Opotow, at the University of Massachusetts Boston, has shown this in her studies of inside-outside attitudes. Being a creative person, she used beetles and research participants.

To begin, she showed everyone a video of the bombardier beetle, a less-than-handsome creature, like Darth Vader with a tobacco-spewing habit. Then Opotow gave different groups of participants different information. She told some that the bombardier was beneficial, saving the agriculture industry a billion dollars a year, and that he made a great father figure—kind of like the human dad who proudly changes diapers.

Other participants heard the opposite—that the bombardier was truly a character with destruction on his mind. Not the dad type, this beetle left his kids in the cornfield to fend for themselves.

Other participants heard other information (good for crops, bad for his kids; bad for crops, good for his kids, and so on), which was all true of some beetle out there somewhere, though not necessarily true about the bombardier. While all participants looked at the same beetle, some eventually perceived him as a social innie and some saw him as a social outie. Needless to say, people who saw the bombardier as an outie were more likely to call the exterminators.

So it comes to this. Opotow's study suggests that how we think about "outsiders" is crucial. We can be the most ordinary, upstanding people, but our invisible perceptions can lead to anything from minor discrimination to full-blown genocide. It helps explain why good people like the Christians in Rwanda can do bad things to fellow Christians when they perceive them as "outside" the scope of justice.

All of this is disturbing to those of us who like to live on the inside and play with suds. Yet my faith, at its core, compels me to examine my thinking regardless of how difficult and embarrassing the process can be. On the bright side, I feel very modern and academic when I realize that I follow a God who is up on the latest beetle research, who seeks to help me grow inside out, who increases not only my scope of justice but also my heart of compassion. I also realize that if my faith had not opened my thinking, I might not be married today—certainly not to the person I'm with, a person of color with South Asian roots. Nor would my beautiful children exist.

I understand that some people don't see the side of Christian faith that opened my heart and gave me an unexpected gift. These people assert that Christianity is based on exclusion, or insider thinking. In certain senses—both historical and theological— they have a point. Nevertheless, I invite them to incline their ears at the door of God's own tent, to listen for the melody of inclusion that began *pianissimo* in the Old Testament only to crescendo to *forte* in the New. This is the major tune that helps us grow beyond our borders.

The tabernacle of Yahweh was crimson, blue and purple. I don't know why, but for years I pictured this glorified tent as an ivory canvas pitched over a camelhair clothesline. This reveals my complete lack of camping-with-the-Israelites knowledge and a late attraction to the book of Exodus.

Now that I know more about the tabernacle, I like to think of it as God's heart—pulsing crimson, blue and purple just beneath its covering of skin. This skin is usually designated in our Bibles as goatskin, but nobody really knows what it was. Just as well. I can simply focus on the status of God's heart.

Before the tabernacle was set among the Israelites, God's heart had been knocking around inside Eden while we wandered around outside, permanently barred from entering. This was not an acceptable situation for a God who created us for communion with himself, a God whose triune nature is the picture of relationship.

Fortunately, God is not discouraged by setbacks and complications. He decided to put his heart in the center of the Israelite community, instructing Moses to build a worship tent according to his heavenly design (see Exodus 26–27). It was a grand inside-out move. Upon the arrival of God's heart among the Hebrews, no one could deny that it was astonishingly beautiful, woven with exquisite thread, whispering love through the lips of pomegranates and golden bells and sprinkling mercy through wings of giant cherubim. Only in generations hence would people notice the promise of our thorn-crowned Jesus that hid in supporting acacia poles—acacia, the thorny desert tree.

At intervals priests entered this exquisite place as if by angioplasty, piped through bloody tubes of animal sacrifice and dark balloons of smoky incense. Once a year the high priest slid all the way in to the mercy seat through a valve of curtain, only to be expelled by a powerful thump. Common people could only imagine what it felt like to be embraced by the inner chambers. And the priests, though privileged to journey inward, could not stay there, near the thrum of God's heart.

Over time it became clear that although God's heart was finally beating in the center of human activity, something had to give. We were still, all of us, coursing on the outside.

The book of John uses an intriguing expression to explain the coming of Jesus. The original language of John 1:14, "The Word became flesh and made his dwelling among us," means that Jesus pitched his tent among us. New Testament writers understood this as an even bolder reality than Israel's holy tabernacle, regarding God's efforts to join us to his heart. They knew that through Jesus, God would make the impossible happen. He would let us enter his exquisite tent of a heart and stay.

By what miracle would God accomplish this? Once I heard it said that Jesus ultimately died of a literal broken heart. I don't know how this would be described in medical terms, or if it is actually possible, but it makes sense—that God provided a way for us to enter his heart by breaking it open like a sacrificial dove torn open on the tabernacle altar (Leviticus 1:17). In fact, Psalm 69 suggests something similar. The psalm, which prefigures Jesus, says, "Scorn has broken my heart" (Psalm 69:20). The Hebrew word for "broken" here means to rend violently, to crush or to rupture.

When I think of the insults that broke Jesus' heart, I'm prone to remember the shame of the cross where, though innocent, he died a criminal's death. But the insults reached much further. First Jesus was exchanged like chattel for Barabbas and sold down the river by his own people, who shouted, "Crucify him!" He was lashed with a flogging whip, stripped in front of soldiers, robed with royal scarlet and crowned with a circlet of thorns (see Matthew 27).

For a scepter he was handed a reed, which he held in his right hand while men knelt before him in mock worship, saying, "Hail, king of the Jews." He was spit on, struck in the head with the mock scepter and stripped again. Though his clothes were eventually returned to him, they were stolen at the foot of the cross. Men gambled for these clothes while Jesus choked in the sun. All the while he hung there—hungry, thirsty and pierced—people passed by and mocked him. Even his own Father averted his glance because Jesus was spattered with our shame and misdeeds.

One could say that by submitting to all these insults Jesus ruptured his own heart, at least figuratively, as Psalm 69 suggests. And the book of Matthew mirrors this rupture in its description of what happened when Jesus died: the earth shook, the rocks split, the temple curtain that separated God's mercy seat from outsiders was rent in two, from top to bottom (Matthew 27:51).

In Ezekiel, God says he will put a new heart in us, one of flesh and not of stone—a Jesus heart, it seems, that brings outsiders in, collapsing the curtains that divide. I believe I've felt the beating of this heart since childhood. Yet it's been a journey to come to terms with its nature. For while God has given me nothing other than his very own heart—his broken, open, inclusive heart—I face a serious question. As this open heart thumps within my soul, I stand by its door and ask: dare I join what God has put asunder?

How thankful I am that as a young adult God did not let me

close the door of my hidden heart to an unexpected, undeserved romantic love. How thankful I am, indeed, that my beloved also let his heart be opened to me. It's good to remember these graces today, even as I face new challenges to live as one who includes and seeks to be included.

9

INDIANA JONES ~ fear

Up from the river's edge, I go to a movie with my new, unexpected love. Here I lean into faux velvet, hold hands in the dark, and watch as Indiana Jones, clothed in common brown, searches for the Holy Grail in his last crusade. He twists through earthen tunnels, tangled cobwebs, the eerie glow of torchlight. The only dragon he must face is fear . . . of death at the hands of his foes, death at the rim of a gaping rock chasm with no bridge, death at the sip of a cup poorly chosen. I hold my breath until a great sigh surges through the crowd. My heart skips a beat, then restarts with relief when Indiana scoops up water with the cup of life and pours it on his father's fatal wounds. Then father and son link eyes and nod the past away.

I like adventure—the kind that gets me on the side of a cliff or speeding across a racetrack at two hundred miles an hour. I like the way this adventure makes my palms sweat and tightens my throat. Life-risking, death-defying, Indiana Jones adventure is just my style. My style, that is, as long as it happens to someone else.

The truth is, with the exception of skiing, writing and helping to raise two lively children, I'm not much for adventure—particularly the life-threatening kind. I never have been. Perhaps this is why I went through a terrible phase after college when all I could think about was death. It seemed to be a grim threat to the relationship I had started to build with my beloved and a fearful question mark blocking our quest for a future. I simply didn't welcome its appearance as part of life. It seemed too risky, too painful, and way too devoid of love and snacks.

That's why, at about this time, I bought a life insurance policy —far before the age that most people would consider such an investment. It's not like I thought the policy would prevent anything, but the mere sound of "insurance" for life had a pleasant ring. I also thought it could somehow be a lasting sign of my affection if left to my beloved in my absence. Thinking back, I suppose this behavior suggests I was not a knight in shining, or even Indiana-brown, armor. I consider, however, that fear of death and loss is a common human emotion.

Such fear, of course, causes a tremendous amount of misplaced effort and stunted growth, not to mention the purchase of too much life insurance. To this, I remember the prophet Jonah. When God said "right," he turned left. When God said "land," he chose sea. When God said "speak," he started to snore. All of this contrarianism was a waste of time and energy; it probably even took a few years off Jonah's life.

I understand, though. I think Jonah was afraid to die. Maybe like me today, when I'm about to board a plane to my next conference or drive to another speaking engagement, he pictured the worst-case scenario and it was pure torture to part with his beloved. Or maybe the thought of losing the embrace of his children for even a day was more than he could bear. I say this despite the fact that Jonah blamed his actions on a different factor—God's compassion toward Nineveh. And I say this despite the fact that Jonah said he was angry enough to die after God spared Nineveh.

My fear-of-death-and-loss theory begins with Jonah's name. It was deceptively frightening, for it meant *dove*, which on the surface seems like a very safe name. The dove, after all, had a reputation for peace work. Noah sent his dove out over the water after the flood and it came back with an olive branch, showing that the earth was at peace once again (see Genesis 8).

Noah's dove mission was not too frightening. It just required stamina and a good set of wings, as peace missions generally do. Indeed, it may have been an inspiration to Jonah that God's Spirit had embarked on a similar peace mission at the dawn of creation. Genesis 1:2 shows God hovering over the dark, watery chaos, and the original language used to describe the event is birdy—the Talmud compares the Spirit in this case to a dove "fluttering."

The problem with dovelike peace work was that it wasn't restricted to water missions. Doves were famous for another peace-making activity, one that was less appealing by far—the kind that happened at the altar when the bird became a sin offering. I'm not saying that Jonah considered this consciously, but the point is, Jonah acted like he knew.

It's hard for me to appreciate the risk of altar sacrifice. I was raised in a culture that purchases birds for food. I see them feather-less, pale and bumpy, sitting silently on pearly Styrofoam. Sometimes there's a little pink water sloshing around under the Saran™ wrap, but for the most part it's a sterile process. We choose a leg, a thigh, a deboned breast and plop it in the cart. The bird sacrifices itself. No struggle. No blood. No fear.

But the Hebrews knew better. They didn't shop at the supermarket for their sacrificial birds. Jonah knew firsthand what happened to doves when they were sacrificed in the peace process. "The priest shall bring it to the altar, wring off the head. . . . Its blood shall be drained out on the side of the altar. . . . He shall tear it open by the wings . . . burn it on the wood that is on the fire" (Leviticus 1:15-17).

Snap, crackle, pop, poof.

I'm not surprised that Jonah didn't share God's perspective on self-sacrifice when God told him to preach to an Assyrian city, an enemy of Israel's. Whether or not Jonah remembered his avian name at this juncture, he absolutely knew that in Assyria he could lose his head or maybe his wings like an altar dove. Maybe he could picture his blood flowing down the walls of Nineveh. Frankly, such an image would set me up for a trip in the opposite direction.

Like Jonah, knowing what could happen, I would have decided that making peace in Tarshish was a better choice. It was a ship's ride away. And besides, doves had a history of over-the-water missions. Why shouldn't Jonah the dove simply follow suit? That's how I would have thought about it, if I were him.

Of course, we know the rest of the story. Jonah fled to the shore where he got on a ship aimed for Tarshish. He probably pocketed all kinds of good intentions for the trip—to preach to Tarshish, to have some adventure, to take a Sabbath rest and eat some snacks.

Well. God had other ideas. He sent a storm while Jonah was in a deep sleep. The sailors, terrified that the ship would sink, shook Jonah out of his slumber and brought him to the lots table—a game of whodunnit played with little rocks. When Jonah got the short end of the stone, so to speak, everyone knew he had done the unthinkable. He was running away from the Big God in a kind of antiquest.

But Jonah faced the dragon anyway. After much futile effort to save his life, the sailors finally threw him overboard right where a sea-dragon, a great fish, was just getting ready for snacktime.

Into the belly of the fish—or possibly the airy laryngeal pouch, as some suppose—Jonah descended. Of this experience he said, "Seaweed was wrapped around my head. / To the roots of the mountains I sank down; / the earth beneath barred me in forever" (Jonah 2:5-6). At the bottom of the sea, at the gates of Hades, Jonah faced the very real possibility of his death. Unable to sleep this time, he prayed for deliverance: "And the LORD commanded the fish, and it vomited Jonah onto dry land" (Jonah 2:10).

This experience equipped the reluctant prophet to take up his proper quest, for he'd come to terms with the fact that death could take him anywhere, anyhow. This knowledge turned him back toward the altar of Nineveh as a dove without promise of permanent head or wings—a peacemaker of the Christ type, on the ground with his enemies to offer re-creation to those who lived outside his heart.

Upon entering Nineveh, he preached the truth with boldness: "'Forty more days and Nineveh will be overturned.' The Ninevites believed God" (Jonah 3:4-5).

This is a happily-ever-after scene if ever there was one, but Jonah missed the delight. After he poured the water of life on his enemies' wounds, reviving them as he was commanded, he waited to see if his enemies would get what they'd deserved before they repented. But God spared the city. So then, in an expression that is nothing less than complete irony, Jonah told God he was angry enough to die.

I could pretend that I don't understand Jonah's ridiculous behavior, but that would require the kind of talk that sells a truck-load of life insurance. The truth is, I understand Jonah all too well. I originally signed up for the Christian life for its protective quali-ties—not thinking it might require trips to Assyria.

So I understand Jonah's initial fear to die at the hands of his enemies and his reticence to see these enemies given mercy. I also understand his ambivalence about living when it finally meant he'd have to coexist with people who wanted to hurt his people. I understand, because there are days when I consider what it would be like to be in Jonah's place—not back in Nineveh, but right here in New York.

For instance, I wonder if my stepfather were still alive how I would react if I had to face him, not knowing if he would seek to harm me. Would my heart be open enough to invite him into my precious faith—the faith that preserved me in his household and beyond? And if by some miracle he accepted the invitation, just as the Ninevites accepted Jonah's warning, would I welcome my step-father into my church? Would I share the cup of life with him— the communion cup of Jesus? Maybe, like Jonah, I would just rather die and put the whole thing behind me. It's hard enough, after all, to simply dredge up the memories.

These thoughts bring Jonah's story forward in time, presenting the real difficulties he must have faced in fulfilling his prophet's quest. In fact, I find a new respect for him, despite all the preaching that casts him in rebellious relief.

To be frank, I quiver to think that we Christians are filled with the same Holy Spirit who sent Jonah to his enemies. And this same Spirit visited Jesus at the Jordan, in the form of a dove, to inaugurate a peace quest that would take him to the cross. How truly brave Jesus was to face the hardness of death and loss, with love and grace to draw him onward. I pray for love and grace to draw me onward too.

10

OLD STONE CHURCH ~ Love

I walk around the old stone church down the road from my postcollege apart-ment. It is like a dream, this sunlit day that has moved in after the previous night of hurricane. And in this way the scene is a parable for me. "The winter is past; the rains are over and gone." Through a veil I watch as three hundred gather, magnolia perfumed, musk shaven. Gingerly holding my father's arm, I watch as people rustle pink chiffon, lemon linen and suits of sorrel wool through towering, weathered doors. In chattering groups they curve into silken cherry pews. Some are looking at the ceiling, the dark mahogany that is carved with lilies and lotuses, a fertile garden twining. The music of Brahms sings past the faces to call me inward. But mostly I hear the voice of my love: "Arise . . . come with me. See! The winter is past; the rains are over and gone."

As a young adult I did not believe in love. No doubt this was directly connected to my parents' enrollment in the long-term multiple-spouse program. In particular I was greatly disillusioned

by the breakup of my father and my piano-playing stepmom
Beezie. It didn't help that he quickly replaced her with someone he
constantly quarreled with, someone we were supposed to embrace
with welcoming hearts.

Needless to say, it irked me to sit in church and watch a couple
vow their endless love. The whole thing seemed like a useless and
hypocritical exercise. I would shift in the pew, beat back the tears
and silently indict them: "Today you agree to become one, but you
will roll like a boulder off a cliff and shatter into a million pieces."
Actually, what I cursed in my mind was probably less coherent and
a whole lot more rude, but that was the spirit of my thoughts.

Not surprisingly I took the long way round to marriage, dating
my beloved for nine years—about half of them rocky—before
finally tying the knot. During the rocky years I tested our love like
a little child tests his parents. I made promises and broke them. I
kept my options open, occasionally going out with other people
despite our status as "going steady." Or I broke off our relationship altogether, acting on my deep need to protect myself from
abandonment.

Through it all, my love did not leave. To me this was inexplicable.
I believed I was worthy of abandonment, based on my past and my
present, yet I remained beloved. I began to feel like Sixo in the novel
Beloved, who said this of his Thirty Mile Woman: "She is a friend of
my mind. She gather me. . . . The pieces I am, she gather them and
give them back to me in all the right order." It was this kind of love,
extended again and again, that brought me to the altar.

To this day some people who attended our wedding still talk
about its wonder. And I think I know what sprinkled delight

throughout that day. My love and I had come through a winter few suspected, and the joy of spring blossomed bright. On the eve of our marriage, at a celebration dinner, my fiancé sang a Michael Card song that recognized this spring. It remains one of my favorites. "Arise my love, my lovely one come. The winter is past and the rains are gone. The flowers appear, it's the season of song."

This is not to say we entered marriage devoid of trouble. Like anyone, we faced and expected the struggle that came with the arrival of spring's song (even today we sometimes trudge through muck). As T. S. Eliot says, "April is the cruelest month, breeding lilacs out of the dead land, mixing memory and desire." We knew that our growth as a couple would depend on the risk of poking through the hard dark, the dead, the pain of what was past and what we longed for. Still, despite the risks of spring we chose it over winter and engraved the reference to this passage in our wedding rings:

> Place me like a seal over your heart,
>   like a seal on your arm;
>   for love is as strong as death,
>   its jealousy unyielding as the grave.
>   It burns like blazing fire,
>   like a mighty flame.
>
> Many waters cannot quench love;
>   rivers cannot wash it away.
>   If one were to give
>   all the wealth of his house for love,
>   it would be utterly scorned. (Song of Songs 8:6-7)

This verse is the culminating cry of the true lovers in the biblical Song of Songs. It is expressed in the voice of the beloved and draws into sharp relief what my love and I had, each in our own way, discovered firsthand: there are two kinds of love—the wintry love of Solomon, which is no love at all, and the true love of the sun-kissed shepherd and shepherdess, which is milk and honey, redemption from the wilderness.

Recently I was delighted to find an interpretation of Song of Songs that, with great clarity, unearths this elusive truth. Iain Provan suggests that the Song, often considered to be a love song between Solomon and his beloved, is actually a poem that contrasts true and false, fertile and unfertile love, setting false Solomon in chiaroscuro with two true lovers.

Brushing carefully through the Song's expressions, Provan notes that the self-seeking love of Solomon splayed itself across "sixty queens and eighty concubines, and maidens without number," while the love of the lovers was set securely each on the other, in passionate, fiery dedication. The desert love of Solomon was planted in Baal Hamon, a vineyard aptly named for the false Canaanite god of fertility, but the love of the lovers was set in a truly fertile garden much like the one in Eden (the presence of pomegranates and mandrakes makes the point). The love of Solomon sacrificed others on the altar of his bed (the feminine word for "coming up" being the same as the word for burnt offering in this case, Song of Songs 3:6), but the love of the lovers was a gentle wooing combined with self-sacrifice.

Further, the love of Solomon rose from a smoky wilderness, coming with coercive, death-dealing power (Song of Songs 3:7-8), while the love of the lovers faced a wilderness together (Song of Songs 8:5), reframing the trauma the beloved experienced when she was taken into Solomon's chambers (notes Provan, the shepherd lover describes the beloved's neck as holding bucklers and shields that were previously the property of Solomon's bodyguards). Thus the love of Solomon is death, but the love of the true lovers overcomes death.

Philip Yancey credits several things for his conversion. One is the kind of transformational, romantic love we see between the true lovers in Song of Songs. This love, says Yancey, "convinced me of the possibility of change in myself. I met a woman who saw worth in me where I had seen little. The hard, cynical shell I had carefully cultivated as a form of protection split apart like a carapace, and to my surprise I discovered that vulnerability need not mean danger."

I was already a Christian when I stumbled on my soul-altering romantic love, so, unlike Yancey, I cannot credit it with bringing me to God. Yet the earthly love that "does not let me go" played and continues to play an enormous role in helping me flourish as it encourages me to unveil the inner chambers of my heart to God. Indeed, above all other natural things, the love I share with my spouse has convinced me that I am lovable to the great I Am, that I can split open my deepest self to him and find a garden of delight and tender safety instead of a wilderness of danger.

Perhaps this is why Song of Songs, Revelation and Hosea intoxicate me so. Whereas some people wait for the day when they can climb into the lap of God the Father, and others ache to lean on his strong shepherd-shoulders, I anticipate the day when God the lover will hold me forever in a passionate and safe embrace.

Interestingly, I've heard a great number of sermons about God my Father and God my shepherd and God my Savior, but I can't remember even one about God my lover who seeks me in a blatant Song of Songs kind of love that brings a person to her knees. It's possible I overslept the day someone talked about God like a Song of Songs lover. Or no one in my circle was ever prompted to deliver that particular sermon. Either way, the result is the same. I'm stepping out of my church experience to speak like this. But I am not stepping out of the Bible.

The very first miracle Jesus performed was at a wedding (see John 2). And even though Jesus admonished his mother for asking him to use his power, saying, "My time has not yet come," he still went ahead and changed water into wine. I find this especially significant. At Cana Jesus was, for a Messiah whom John painstakingly portrays as being in complete control of timing, uncharacteristically ready to do this miracle before the "fullness of time." It seems to me Jesus saw a priceless opportunity to show us why he had come—one reason being his plan to wed us in love. This is suggested by the setting of the miracle and is spoken of in Hosea, Ephesians and Revelation.

In Revelation and Ephesians, Jesus is specifically pictured as our marriage partner, hearkening back to the ancient promise in Hosea. There God makes a beautiful declaration: he will tenderly call us out of the wilderness, the valley of disaster, into the vineyard of his love (Hosea 2:14-16). When we walk through the valley's "door of hope" into his chambers, we are made to "lie down in safety" (Hosea 2:15, 18).

At this point I remember Song of Songs, where the true lovers slip past the veil to an inner chamber, and all that happens in that safe space is spice and fruit and perfume. There, wrapped in fidelity, the shepherd and shepherdess drink of each other in a sort of spiced wine, milk and honey escapade. I daresay they bring each other to their knees.

At the end of time, I know we'll all be brought to our knees before Jesus. While some will buckle in disgrace, I rather expect the moment will be a taste of hot wine, frothy milk and jasmine honey, explosive enough to set me reeling and babbling. I also expect it to be more of what I already experience with God; my pieces will be gathered and given back to me in the right order.

Whether I can capture and communicate this hidden grace to others may depend on my vineyard-tending habits. For as the true lovers note in the Song, there are "little foxes" all around (Song of Songs 2:15), scouting the place for the slightest breach in fences.

11

ΓoLDsworthy's waLL ~ sacrifice

About an hour up the river is an outdoor art center. I take my little children and so decide not to cross the five hundred acres on foot. Instead we board an open-air shuttle, which will toil past towering granites, bolted iron sculptures and a molded bonfire of shredded tires reaching to the blue. The air is scented with new-mown hay. In the thick of summer's bustle we barely glimpse a stone wall that drops off into green water——some farmer's error, so it seems. Later, back in the cool of the gift shop, we see a book that talks about the wall. The photos, especially those taken during winter's want, transform our view . . . beneath stripped trees a stone-gray body slithers wide arcs across the sprawling landscape. Or maybe the wall is a dragon's tail, hiding in the forest, while the creature itself hibernates beneath the silence of a frozen pond.

Landscape artist Andy Goldsworthy plays with sticks and stones, thorns and rushes, winding creeks and lazy ponds. He is a grown man. But like a child he sees possibility in every fallen branch. When I encounter a piece like Goldsworthy's stone wall, I wake up to the work of God. There I remember that he played in the dirt at creation, even kissing the dust with his living breath. Similarly, Jesus made mud pies to feed the eyes of the blind man. And the Holy Spirit is building a path of living stones, his people—a swish of gray and ordinary grace across the landscape.

Even so, I often hesitate to join God when he's working with his people; I'm reluctant to roll up my sleeves, press my fingers into sand, place stone on stone. Maybe I am still more wounded than I think, hesitant to invest myself in others, to give myself fully like my mother did, fearing I'll end up with nothing. Or maybe, in a kind of selfish pride, I prefer the Master side of God better than the Child, so I look for the big ministry opportunities while neglecting hundreds of opportunities presented every day—in the fields of my common relationships.

In my worst moments, I even view the ordinary relationships of life as obstacles to my fulfillment and achievements. It was like this when my first daughter was born. Sure I gave birth to her. Yes I loved her. But I had a teaching career, a job that people respected. How could I give that up to stay home? I had no intentions of making such a sacrifice.

So my spouse and I paid the deposit at a local daycare center and waved goodbye to our seven-month-old Sara. She would be well cared for in that place with its lemon-yellow walls, video cameras and hands that changed diapers wearing rubber gloves. I was sad on one level but relieved to "get my life back," as I'd heard women say with the same tone when discussing postpregnancy weight loss. "I want my body back," they'd say.

But then my infant daughter made her own plea: "I want my

mommy back." At seven months old she had no words to say this. She simply stopped eating in my absence. The daycare workers were frantic. Babies don't refuse to eat for ten hours straight. When I would retrieve Sara from their arms, she'd be dazed and unresponsive. She ignored my attempts to communicate with her. My lively, smiley baby was gone.

After two straight weeks of this we took Sara to the doctor, who asked us, "Has something changed in Sara's life? Babies who are distressed sometimes go on hunger strikes." I went home that day knowing I was at a crossroads. My daughter wanted me, but I wanted a life. What's more, I wanted a house. With my salary, we were on track to get one soon—a good-sized home in which to raise a family.

The apostle Paul says, "Whatever you do, whether in word or deed, do it all in the name of the Lord Jesus" (Colossians 3:17). This statement precedes a passage that discusses the importance of ordinary relationships—spouse to spouse, child to parent and so forth. In this way Paul was asking me to change my perspective. He wanted me to get on my knees and steady the living stones that shared my space in the wall, to kick off my shoes and follow where the wall dropped off into green waters. He wanted me to sacrifice my desires for Sara's pleas.

I like the way Mark Strom discusses Paul's message. The Christian life is not, he says, painted in the colors of special rituals or holy texts; rather it is built with dabs of person-to-person interaction, a "set of relationships." Thus "God communicate[s] himself [to Christians] not primarily through the written word and tradition or mystical experience and cultic activity, but through one another." We could add that this is how God primarily communicates to the world—through the common love of Christians as they move in relationship.

This makes sense to me, much as I love books and traditions, songs and rituals. It makes sense that God enters the world most powerfully through strong, loving, giving and forgiving relationships. After all, God is really a relationship in orbit, three persons in perpetual motion with each other: Father, Son and Holy Spirit. And God started everything on earth with two people—Adam and Eve in the first image-of-God orbital relationship.

In fact, Satan must have sensed that relationships had the power to light up the universe. For he wasted no time stirring strife into the first relationships. With one tempting ingredient—the desire for knowledge outside of relationship—he attacked the sinews that connected Adam to Eve, humanity to God, and humanity to the rest of creation.

I believe that by launching this offensive, Satan tried to attack the very heart of God with hopes that he'd destroy it. I imagine his delight when God turned Adam and Eve out of the garden. Perhaps he thought this was the end of relationship, even the end of God, the demise of his very nature. I also imagine his shock much later, when God opened the way back to Eden through an act of relationship. When Jesus gave his life in exchange for his beloved ones, the dry bones of relationship jumped and clattered, reconnected and grew flesh (Ezekiel 37:5-14). God's nature prevailed.

As God's nature prevailed in heaven, with relationship remaining front and center, so I'm asked to let it prevail on earth. I remember, sometimes with a grumpy sigh, that Paul raises common love far beyond my achievements, accumulations or agendas, saying,

> If I speak in the tongues of men and of angels, but have not
> love, I am only a resounding gong or a clanging cymbal. If I
> have the gift of prophecy and can fathom all mysteries and all
> knowledge, and if I have a faith that can move mountains, but
> have not love, I am nothing. If I give all I possess to the poor
> and surrender my body to the flames, but have not love, I
> gain nothing. (1 Corinthians 13:1-3)

Sara, now long past babyhood, recently fashioned this truth into
a simple declaration. She was in her room and I could hear her and
her sister Sonia playing with their dolls, who happened to be
attending some kind of church function. Things were getting testy
between the toys—maybe they were discussing a controversial
theological point. I couldn't be sure, but I heard Sara speak pas-
sionately. "Well!" she said, "In church, we're not just connected
with pins and staples. We're connected by love. If it's not like that,
then what's the point?"

If I do not have love, I am nothing. If the church does not have
love, it is nothing. What's the point? Martin Luther King Jr.
broadly challenged his listeners on this question in his sermon
"The Three Dimensions of a Complete Life":

> Oh, there will be a day, the question won't be "How many
> awards did you get in life?" Not on that day. (Yeah.) It won't
> be "How popular were you in your social setting?" That
> won't be the question on that day. (Yeah.) . . . The question
> that day will not be "How beautiful is your house?" (That's
> right.) The question that day will not be "How much money

did you accumulate? How much did you have in stocks and bonds?" . . . On that day the question will be "What did you do for others?" (That's right.)

Or maybe on that day Jesus will speak to each of us much as he spoke to Peter. Maybe he will meet us over a fish breakfast, look us in the eye and say, "Did you love me? Did you tend my sheep? Did you care for my children?" (see John 21:17).

Tending sheep is a mundane job. It is a lot of same old, same old—the way we feed kids breakfast, lunch and dinner, or drive to the office and deal with the same people day after day. It is repetitive, like building a stone wall rock by rock across the landscape. So it's easy for us to overlook the power of small acts that are folded again and again into the meandering swish of common love.

Recently I sat across the table from a friend who does all sorts of mundane tasks. She drives her daughter to eight specialist appointments a week. She feeds her family. She and her husband are opening their arms to a new baby from another country.

As we sat at our corner table, this woman raised her cup and sipped. Then with much earnestness, she said, "I just wish I could do something for the Lord."

I'm not the type to get sappy over tea. But when she said this, I just about spit out my scone. It took a second before I could speak.

"It hurts so much to hear you say that," I told her. I mentioned all the sheep-tending I knew she did on a daily basis, as well as her plans to do more with a newborn. "Not to minimize your desire," I ventured, "but hearing you say this reminds me of the woman who anointed Jesus before his burial. Who was she, really? What big life did she have? Yet for the mundane act of pouring her perfume on Jesus to prepare him for death she's remembered wherever the gospel is shared."

In heaven's eyes, the woman's mundane act was so royally beautiful that Jesus chose to memorialize it forever. To Jesus, who was approaching death, the woman who anointed him was greater than the richest Hollywood starlet. So too my friend is a rich gift to her family, a shepherd given them for life's journey. No one is going to put her on TV for what she does every day. She will never be an *American Idol* star.

Because the rewards are quiet, being dependable in common love is not always inviting. The reward of putting rock on rock isn't always visible. Sometimes the work is dirty. We get scraped and bored. We don't always see the wall of grace we're building for the Lord.

That's how I felt when I stood at the crossroads with my daughter saying in her baby way, "Mommy, come home." To me, the field looked empty. The work looked messy. The days stretched out into endless boredom. No one would make me an *Idol* star if I quit my job to tend my home.

But God's Spirit was like a wintry wind that came along and stripped the trees to show me the wall-building project I'd be up to. He spoke quietly on my way back from work: "You can have a big house with nothing to put in it. Or you can give up the job and the house and fill your home with love." While God doesn't necessarily ask every woman to leave work for a child, he seemed to be urging me in that direction and graciously promising, "I will make . . . your walls of precious stones" (Isaiah 54:12).

As it went, I took him at his word.

12

cLefts of tHe ROCK ~ ResPONSIBILity

When I look out across this river, I see the cliffs and mountains that shelter a special place . . . a house I loved to go to as a child. Inside its walls, pickles and jellies poured off shelves and pies marched from an ancient oven—cherry, apple, rhubarb, peach. On its property, berries swelled into round moons of pleasure. Vines curled, climbed in the clefts of rock walls. Trees swayed and bowed, dropping fruits into my eager hands. I stained my lips purple with mulberries, dirtied my nails digging potatoes, tripped through golden grasses chasing tiny blue butterflies. My grandmother rose early to care for this place, donning denim overalls and shading her face with a wide straw hat. She sweated dark circles around her neck and armpits, perched red-faced on tower-ing ladders to prune and shape. She combed the lake in her rowboat, lifting lily pads like fainted water nymphs to build a pyre of amber green beneath the flames of the sun.

The life of kings has always fascinated me—all that pomp and glory, personal tailors and cooks, dancing girls and flutes, snacks any time of the day or night. Not that I risk falling into this life anytime soon, but I sometimes wonder, would I be a good king or a bad king if I had the choice? Would I play the hardworking shepherd like my grandmother, or would I be the bedbound royal? Would I go out and survey my vineyards, or would I fade into laziness, trusting the security of my fences to chance or servants?

In the Song of Songs I discover that I needn't be of royal position to face these questions. As I listen to the common shepherd and shepherdess mourn their failure (he roughly rattles the lock, she refuses to get out of bed—Song of Songs 5:3-4, 6-7), and as I watch them gaze anxiously on their future, crying out, "Catch for us . . . the little foxes / that ruin the vineyards" (Song of Songs 2:15), I remember that questions of how to live face everyone.

We are each like little kings privileged with a patch of ground, even if it's less than a quarter-acre, like mine, and more likely to grow dandelions than a vineyard. We each hold a scepter of influence. And we each exist in the narrow "clefts of the rock" like the Song's lovers (Song of Songs 2:14)—in relationship to someone, or a group of people, or even God, who all spy eagerly to see what our face and voice will reveal. We are each, to put it simply, responsible in our blessedness. Whether or not we let temptations woo us into irresponsibility is up to us.

This was put to me straight by my eldest daughter, Sara, when she was a mere five years old. I'd been teaching our two girls that life is full of privileges, and that with these privileges come responsibilities. The idea was that if the children failed to act responsibly regarding a privilege, they'd lose it. Okay. So one day I was yelling at the kids to get in the car. I was still picking at them once they finally settled in. Sara piped up from the back seat. "You know, with privilege comes responsibility."

I knew right away what she meant. Never mind that I had made a sacrifice in the past, quitting my job to tend my vineyard at home. Today I was being lazy about the upkeep. I hadn't appreciated the privilege of children enough to act responsibly regarding their emotional needs. "Are you saying that someone should take my children away?" I asked Sara. She just grinned with that knowing look children sometimes conjure. But still, I felt the threat of loss.

In such moments I often balk and create excuses for my behavior. I call on memories to justify myself, thinking, "At least I'm not choking my children the way my stepfather tried to choke my sister! At least I'm not brandishing a knife and screaming wildly, the way my mother did to make my stepfather unhand her. I'm not using foul language. I'm not throwing my dinner plate clear across the kitchen. And even if I did—who could blame me? Look how my family taught me to face the challenges of relationship."

Yet God's Word doesn't have immunity clauses. Regardless of my background, the Scripture speaks soberly to me about privilege, responsibility and consequent loss. In Matthew, Jesus likens God to a king who, at the judgment, says to those at his right hand, "Come . . . take your inheritance, the kingdom prepared for you. . . . For I was hungry and you gave me something to eat, I was thirsty and you gave me something to drink, I was a stranger and you invited me in, I needed clothes and you clothed me, I was sick and you looked after me, I was in prison and you came to visit me" (Matthew 25:34-36).

Then he turns to those at his left and says, "Depart from me, you who are cursed, into the eternal fire prepared for the devil and his angels. For I was hungry and you gave me nothing to eat, I was thirsty and you gave me nothing to drink" (Matthew 25:41-42). As far as I can tell, a crowd forgot that with privilege comes responsibility, and because of their lapse they lost heaven. This is a hard message but not necessarily negative. There are times when threat speaks most persuasively to my hardened heart.

For more positive inspiration, however, I'm glad I can thank my grandmother. She faithfully caught the "little foxes" on her property —not out of fear, but out of a deep desire to delight the ones with whom she shared a space in the clefts of the rock. Memories of her land and her pantry quicken my desire to live in godly responsibility to others, particularly to my children. When I think of my grandmother's blueberries, raspberries and currant berries folded into rich jams, her pies that were fat with hand-stoned cherries, her willows and pear trees that swung shadows onto our lakeside path, such abundance calls out. It invites me to care for my own vineyard with great attentiveness. This takes sacrificial discipline, and sometimes it takes temporary emptiness and want.

Back in the time of the Israelites, God had a novel way of building discipline, emptiness and want into the lives of his people. He mandated the Sabbath—once every week, once every seven years, once every fifty years (see Exodus 20:9-10; Leviticus 25:3-4, 8-10). These Sabbaths each had specific purposes, but I believe they also functioned to teach us what my grandmother knew: emptiness, want and discomforting discipline are channels through which bounty can ultimately flow.

After all, looking back to the seventh-day Sabbath, we see that a vacuum of work prepared minds and bodies for productivity. And in the seventh-year Sabbath, we see that letting the land lie empty prepared the ground to burst forth with produce. Finally, on the fifty-year Sabbath, we find that the discipline of turning over accumulated slaves and property could prepare the heart to remember who really owned the "cattle on a thousand hills" (Psalm 50:10), ultimately deepening dependence on God.

To help us get the point with greater clarity, God sent Jesus to live among us. Jesus was our Sabbath in action, emptying himself to come here, releasing his right to godhood. He disciplined himself to walk a path of deconstruction to ultimately become the cornerstone of a construction project that continues to this day. I search for ways to bring what he did as a living Sabbath into my experience and understanding. I try to explore the paradoxical truth regarding the empty path to fullness in language I can understand.

Annie Dillard speaks to me. She talks about writing like it's a building project. She knows that sometimes one must take the empty path, the road of deconstruction, to create what is sound and full. Says Dillard,

> The line of words is a hammer. You hammer against the walls of your house. You tap the walls lightly everywhere. After giving many years' attention to these things, you know what to listen for. Some of the walls are bearing walls; they have to stay, or everything will fall down. Other walls can go with impunity; you can hear the difference. Unfortunately, it is often a bearing wall that has to go. It cannot be helped. There

is only one solution, which appalls you, but there it is. Knock it out. Duck.

As a writer I've felt the collapse of hope in that moment when I tear down what I thought was best to build, or what I was tempted to build out of vanity or ignorance. Yet I also know the joy of seeing something truer arise from the emptiness, something that speaks to the heart of those who walk around inside my words. This truth, experienced through writing, can inform my understanding of the paradoxical Sabbath truth: emptiness, want and discomforting discipline can lead to fullness.

Still, it's not easy to take the empty road—not as a writer, a spouse, a parent, a friend. In a society that gluts itself with dancing girls, flutes and snacks any time of the day or night, it's not easy to stand arm in arm with empty air while everyone around me looks so full and royal. Very little in society teaches me to be like my Sabbath-Jesus. Much tempts me to cling to the illusion of promise.

The Chinese have a wonderful tale that speaks to my dilemma. In *The Empty Pot* I meet an emperor who is looking for his successor. He sets a contest—to see who can grow the most beautiful flower. But he provides the seeds. One child, Ping, has always excelled at making things grow. But his seed doesn't germinate. He waters it, puts it in the sun, feeds it good things. His pot remains empty.

On the appointed day all the children of the kingdom bring their pots to the emperor. Out of bold porcelains rise white daisies, purple pansies, fuchsia zinnias and red poppies. Yet Ping comes downcast, holding an empty pot. The emperor takes an interest in Ping, listens to his story of woe, then turns to the other children and says, "Where you got your seeds from, I do not know.

For the seeds I gave you had all been cooked. . . . I admire Ping's great courage to appear before me with the empty truth, and now I reward him with my entire kingdom and make him Emperor of all the land." The doubtful path turned out to be the road to royalty.

Sometimes I understand the truth of this tale as if I've heard it whispered all my life. In these moments I tend my vineyard with resolve and grace, the way my grandmother tended her land. I'm kind to my spouse, nurturing to my children, dependable to my friends and the world. Yet more often than I wish I embody the child who plants counterfeit seeds in bawdy porcelain and loses the kingdom. In these moments I forget my responsibility to trim past temptations into empty air. I forget that this doubtful space is where the glow of purple clusters can burst forth—round moons of pleasure, fit for a king or a commoner.

13

oLive press ~ gratituDe

*At the end of the day, when my children are sleeping, I like to read in bed
and face the river. Today I am reading* The Swallows of Kabul. *I'm
drawn to its cover . . . sky blue, a swirl of peace. But I turn the pages to find
a city lost and afraid, where carved doors hang from hinges, rusted, in decay.
At the city's outskirts, guns "exchang[e] shatter prayers," claiming empty air.
In Kabul one can rise out of vague existence by lowering others into the
execution hole. A comforting simplicity enfolds the process. Just bind thighs
and arms with care. Push a rag into the mouth, eclipse the pleading voice.
Then drop a veil to blind the eyes. Create a corpse even before the first stone
flies. Still. The prisoner's mind works, terrified. Free ears hear the holy man's
judgment drift out over the scratch of stones being gathered. On the light side
of the veil, common rocks begin to raise old men, young men, small boys out
of agitation. Before them, under the hard arc of punishment, a silent body
shudders, quivers in the darkness until a "red stain blossoms" on blue cloth.
The prisoner pays the cost.*

If I've heard it once, I've heard it a thousand times—from the pulpit week after week, in Bible studies, at prayer meetings, even, on occasion, before slicing the birthday cake for the next over-the-hiller among us. "Thank you, Jesus, for dying on the cross, for paying the price for our sins." It can be almost mechanical, an expected prayer uttered as a kind of club ritual.

Sometimes I wonder if anyone hears it at all. Feels faint or sweaty when the words "pay the price" tumble into the air. I admit that as this prayer of gratitude floats out over bowed heads, looking for a resting place, it often drifts right over mine. When I notice it sigh past me, I feel like I'm missing something—a big event. After all, this prayer is the very center of my faith. It is the remembrance that my Sabbath-Jesus emptied himself to step into the stoning hole for me.

I question my lack of response. When this prayer drifts by, why do I sit there distracted—thinking instead about the latest book I added to my Amazon wish list, or silently cursing someone's annoying lily perfume, or predicting whether the birthday cake is chocolate or carrot?

Thinking of my gardening grandma gives me some ideas. There was a time when she delighted to simmer and bake us into euphoria. We walked into her dining room like stick figures but trudged into the living room, plump, by the time she snuffed the candles. She had many tools with which to fatten us, but one of her best was a German apple cake.

Last year our daughter wanted an apple cake recipe at Christmastime. I could taste the memory of Grandma's apple cake like it was already on my tongue. So I placed a call to my father to see if he could get Grandma to share the recipe. You'd think she'd never eaten apple cake in her life. She just shrugged her shoulders and said, "I don't know any apple cake."

The stride of years had shed all memory of her famous cake along the way. And I knew that because she forgot the cake, she couldn't taste it on her tongue like I could. She couldn't picture the dark crust hiding chunks of sweet, soft apple. She couldn't recall the smell of roasted cinnamon. She didn't feel the need for a cup of strong black tea with cream when my father talked apple cake with her.

I'm not about to compare Jesus to an apple cake. But I realize when thinking of my grandmother that, for you and me, a stretch of years as a Christian can produce a similar forgetfulness. Over time we can lose a taste for how sweet and beautiful is Jesus' gift of "paying the price." Drinking milk and honey for many years can make us forget we once had only bread and water. Standing in the light for so long, we forget the terror of being bound in veiled darkness.

This, of course, leads us into temptation. We're tempted to forget who we are without Jesus. We pat ourselves on the back for our grace and strength and reason that we're really not bad people at all. Suddenly Jesus' decision to die in our place seems a little excessive; we've forgotten why we were condemned to step into the stoning hole in the first place. Piously overconfident and apathetic about spreading the good news of Jesus, we own a lot of classy Christian clothes, but the label inside says "Pharisee."

I can't say I find it easy to step out of this apparel. But sometimes I close my eyes and become a translator. I take my private angers, lustful fantasies, derogatory thoughts and so on, and I translate them into marks or bruises or postures. I pretend that the invisible indiscretions in my head are having a criminal, visible effect on the people around me.

Suddenly, my angry impulses produce bruises on my spouse's face, lashes on my children's arms. My fantasies leave an acquaintance lying in the mud, clothes torn, skin scraped. My lingering disillusionments with parents and stepparents break their bones. My own head becomes battered from all my hurtful thoughts. And this is just a week's worth of translation. I imagine a month, a year, and realize my translation has accumulated into a death and a burial. I face the electric chair for translated murder, and suffer fatal complications from translated self-injury.

When I think of how people describe relational pain, this exercise doesn't seem so far off. After all, we say things like, "She cut me to the heart." "He wounded me." "She stepped all over me." "He crushed me." "She left me in the dirt." "He's killing me." "She stripped me of my dignity."

I also remember that Jesus was a translator. He said that if I even look at someone with lust, I've already committed adultery with that person in my heart. If I'm angry with my brother, I'm guilty of murder. If I call my brother a fool, I'm in danger of the fires of hell (see Matthew 5:21-28). He knows what's going on inside me, so he looks at my mind and heart and translates for me.

What I find remarkable is that he doesn't quit there; instead, he goes a step further and translates again. My secret violence moves from imagined marks on me and mine to actual lashes on his own body. "He was pierced for [my] transgressions, / he was crushed for [my] iniquities / . . . by his wounds [I am] healed" (Isaiah

53:5). My hidden violence becomes a forgiven secret, manifested on his flesh without my name attached. I catch my breath to think of it.

If I lived in a different society, say that of ancient Israel or a place with *sharia* law, I think I'd feel the import of Jesus' gift more keenly. If for my transgressions I faced the possibility of losing a hand or an eye, or if I faced being carted off to a stoning hole, how much sweeter I might find his gift of substitution.

In fact, when I sat to read *The Swallows of Kabul*, I felt more thankful for Jesus' gift than I had in a long time. As I saw the "red stain blossom" across blue cloth, I felt that I was beneath the bloodied burqa. I sensed the rocks hitting like punches. So when a thought pushed into my consciousness as if the voice of Jesus were saying, "I would go there. I would step into the stoning hole," this struck me as hard as any story about the cross.

The thought of God stepping into a stoning hole unearthed something deep in my heart—a buried desire to be loved unswervingly. Perhaps this is the hidden desire of every person. But it's surely a raw desire in someone like me, a person let down by family members who were responsible to love or protect but often did not. In any case, thinking of Jesus in a stoning hole caused me to see things afresh and transported me from Golgotha to Gethsemane.

Many people imagine Gethsemane as the olive garden where three figures met—Jesus, the Father and Satan (see Matthew 26:36-46). Yet after reading *Swallows*, I saw a fourth figure in the shadows, draped with a dirty burqa, awaiting execution in a pit dug near the stones of an olive press. Looking at the press and the dark hole in the ground, I felt my heart crush within me. I realized that the veiled figure was me and you—the unfaithful bride of God, condemned to the pit because she dared to make a deal with it (Isaiah 28:15). I could hear the chant of the holy man's judgment coming from the ancient book of the Law: "Stone her to death, because she committed a disgraceful act in Israel by prostituting herself in her father's house" (Deuteronomy 22:21 NRSV). The song of Isaiah drifted through the leaves: "Terror and pit and snare / await you, O people of the earth" (Isaiah 24:17).

I saw Jesus on his knees, faltering between choices. Should he step into the hole and set the woman free, or let her be trampled by stones of judgment? Satan came to Jesus and whispered the Father's words from Hosea: "Ephraim is oppressed, crushed in judgment, / because he was determined to go after vanity. . . . [He] has given bitter offense, / so his Lord will bring his crimes down on him" (Hosea 5:11; 12:14 NRSV). Then, with an air of triumph, Satan turned to the veiled figure and said, "The ransom for a life is costly, / no payment is ever enough" (Psalm 49:8).

It was a terrible moment. Jesus knew the truth and he knew the lie. There was a price that could be offered. In his plea to the Father, "May this cup be taken from me" (Matthew 26:39), I heard him breathe the lament of David: "What I did not steal / must I now restore?" (Psalm 69:4 NRSV). He made this plea three times after coming and going, hoping beyond hope.

But at the last I saw a new look in the eyes of Jesus. He cried out to the condemned, "How can I give you up, Ephraim? / How can I hand you over, O Israel? / . . . My heart recoils within me; my compassion grows warm and tender" (Hosea 11:8 NRSV). Then Jesus lifted the soiled burqa off the figure and replaced it with his own clean cloak. He whispered through her tangled hair, "For you I was born. Though you've walked in darkness, now you've seen a great light. You who walked in deep darkness, on you light has shined. Now you are ransomed. Return to Zion with singing and everlasting joy upon your head" (see Isaiah 9:2, 6; 35:10).

It was like a strange marriage ceremony—the groom left holding the veil, his bride fleeing into the night. And it wasn't just any veil he held while his groomsmen swooned under the olive trees. It was the burqa of his condemned beloved, which the Father placed over his head before setting him into the stoning hole to live, and die, his vows in silence.

I sit on the fringes of this grace-filled scene while the tune of some over-the-hiller's Happy Birthday rises with the dawn. The ritual prayer of gratitude circles back and finds me ready. It lands gently on my head, and I choke out a quiet echo, "Thank you, Jesus, for paying the price for my sins."

Clothed afresh in gratitude, I'm ready to run. To healing, to truth, to an outward life, to the future.

14

forest star ~ humility

Most nights I do not remember my dreams. I drift to sleep after Venus rises over the river, and my mind remains in darkness until morning pushes its way past room-darkening shades. Most nights. But this night I dream in muted colors of earth and stone and towering, moss-covered pines. I am in the dream, standing on a thick carpet of bronzed needles, and I am outside the dream, watching through filtered light and shadow. My back is to me, hidden by long chestnut curls. I watch myself dig into pockets and pull out round, gray stones. A silent crowd stands shoulder to shoulder nearby, shifting now this way, now that as they watch me begin to toss the pebbles. Each pebble sails through the air and lands with a barely perceptible "thop" in the center of a stone enclosure built like a sturdy farmer's wall but in the shape of a star. It will take a long time to fill this empty space, but I am tossing.

I'm so different from my eldest daughter. While I dream of building myself a star monument before the crowds, she plans to cast herself in humble cardboard media. For the sake of her artistic vision our family collects toilet paper rolls. Little gray tubes lurk in every corner of the house. They laze beneath beds. Up in the attic they're bundled in white plastic bags; more rolls lounge between Shakespeare volumes and an old yellow Teletubby.

I muse about why Sara is willing to portray herself so humbly and why I am so needy for a star monument in my honor. No doubt some of the difference is due to personality, some to artistic preference. But I also think back to a conversation I had in the car with my father not long before he married his fifth wife.

We sailed down an exit ramp, then sat idling in the dark. My father turned right on red and broke the news. Another marriage, this one good and right. I was still grieving his pending divorce from his fourth wife. And I could see it now: more photographs to either hide from my children or explain. I could hear them asking, "Who's that, Mommy?" But more than this, there was the child in me. I swallowed and said quietly, "I'm afraid to lose you again, to another woman and her children."

He reassured me, and truly my new stepmother has been nothing but kind. Still, the reality is that I'm not at the center of two people's unified love the way my daughter is. I'm one of a crowd of eighteen siblings, most of whom were picked up by my father's marriages. These siblings occupy his memories and energies. They occupy his time and resources. Some of them reside in his heart.

Perhaps it's no surprise, then, that I have strange dreams of being honored with a stone star monument. Deep inside, I think I want proof that I'm worthy of lavish love and attention no one can ask me to share. This makes me especially vulnerable to the temptation to garner attention. More often than I should, I hand out pebbles like candy, waiting for those around me to toss their contributions into my empty star. I am not proud of this behavior. However, I take comfort that I'm in good company.

In his journal Thomas Merton wrote,

> Someone accused me of being a "high priest" of creativity. Or, at least, of allowing people to regard me as one. This is perhaps true.
>
> The sin of wanting to be a pontiff, of wanting to be heard, of wanting converts, disciples. Being in a cloister, I thought I did not want this. Of course I did, and everyone knows it.
>
> St. William, says the Breviary this night, when death approached, took off his pontifical vestments (what he was doing with them on in bed I can't imagine) and by his own efforts got to the floor and died.
>
> So I am like him, in bed with a miter on. What am I going to do about it?
>
> I have got to face the fact that there is in me a desire for survival as pontiff, prophet, and writer, and this has to be renounced before I can be myself at last.

Reading this passage of Merton's makes me think of Moses—a man who, like me, probably had esteem issues due to his early life experiences. Yet regardless of his understandable weaknesses, when Moses, who was a prophet and a pontiff if there ever was one, hit the rock in the desert instead of commanding it to yield water, God was swift to de-vest him.

Moses had stood before the rock and shouted to the people in grand style, "Listen, you rebels, must we bring you water out of this rock?" (Numbers 20:10). Then he struck the rock twice with his staff and water gushed out. Moses probably felt very impressive in that moment, doing his thing, getting results, watching the commoners splash around in his good work.

But God cut around the big-boy stuff and spoke to Moses: "Because you did not trust in me enough to honor me as holy in the sight of the Israelites, you will not bring this community into the land I give them" (Numbers 20:12). One self-aggrandizing moment and now Moses would die this side of the Promised Land after spending almost forty years trying to get into it.

I always thought it was unfair of God to keep Moses from crossing over just because he hit the rock for water. After all, this prophet had lived through a lot; he'd been an amazing leader for a long, long time. He had done great things for God. And he had the excuse of a difficult past.

But reading Merton's line about his own need to renounce the desire for greatness, I suddenly wonder if God's decision wasn't an act of pure grace. I envision it differently now, as God helping Moses take his miter off, helping him get to the floor and die, reminding him that just because he'd talked to God and used the power of God didn't mean he'd become God. Perhaps God's decision opened the way for Moses to be himself again—just a man— so that he could be remembered in honor, the special kind that says here was a person who communed with God, who stood in the center of his love.

Not long after the rock incident, at the end of Moses' life, God showed him the Promised Land and reminded him that he would not enter. It's a poignant scene: a tired old man standing on the brink of blessing, looking into the green, the dust of the desert stinging his eyes and stirring his regret. But at the last, grace bil-lows into the scene through these words: "No prophet has risen in Israel like Moses, whom the LORD knew face to face" (Deuteron-omy 34:10).

In this final moment I get the feeling that God de-vested Moses, kept him out of the Promised Land, so he could keep him at breath's length—no miter, no mask between him and his beloved prophet. Face to face, breath to breath, no veil between them, God helped Moses keep what he almost forfeited—the loving glory of the Lord.

Paul calls this freedom. He says, "And we, who with unveiled faces all reflect the Lord's glory, are being transformed into his likeness with ever-increasing glory" (2 Corinthians 3:18). When we are face to face with God, his glory shines all over us and out from us like sunshine. This glory surpasses anything we could mus-ter through our own personal candlelight and showers us with lav-ish love.

So why do we raise the veil between our faces and God's glory by seeking attention for ourselves? Maybe it is, after all, a failure of trust (as God told Moses, "Because you did not trust in me . . ."). Perhaps we're afraid that if we don't drum up a little admiration, we'll be lost, outshone, like a child who is one of eighteen siblings. I understand this. It is also the mistake of Absalom.

Absalom was King David's third son, and he wanted to shine. When I watch him I feel his desires percolating under my own skin. For at the city gate, as people came bringing their cases to the king, he sat thinking, "If only I were appointed judge in the land! Then everyone who has a complaint or case could come to me and

I would see that he gets justice" (2 Samuel 15:4). As the people came near, he put out his hand, took hold of them and kissed them. "So he stole the hearts of the men of Israel" (2 Samuel 15:6).

It is tempting to steal people's hearts, to add them to our personal collection, to use them as stones in a memorial we build for ourselves, especially if we're working for a good cause along the way. Absalom did that; he built himself greatness, one heart at a time, even as he served the people. Absalom also set up a pillar for himself in the King's Valley, though he was not king. Eventually his desires led him to do the unconscionable; he tried to take over his father's throne by leading a rebellion. His desires for praise led him down a dark path where he battled the one who had given him life, talent and position.

In classic, straight-faced irony, the Bible sums up the outcome of Absalom's battle with his father: "The casualties that day were great" (2 Samuel 18:7). And, "They took Absalom, threw him into a big pit in the forest and piled up a large heap of rocks over him" (2 Samuel 18:17). The implications could not be worse. Everything he hoped to gain was lost—the kingship, the glory, even the simple honor of a marked grave.

I can't help but see the parallels between Absalom's tragic end and the fate of the Evil One described in Isaiah. Lucifer, who is called the Day Star, also sought to shine brighter than the true King. Isaiah recounts, "O Day Star, son of Dawn! / . . . You said in your heart / . . . 'I will make myself like the Most High.' / But you are brought down to Sheol, / to the depths of the Pit" (Isaiah 14:12-15 NRSV). Both Absalom and Satan find their end in a pit.

Removed from true glory, not even a flicker of their candlelight breaks into the darkness.

So I find that my temptations for glory put me in very bad company. Absalom, Satan—starmongers of the worst sort, father-fighters in their hidden hearts. With my pebbles in hand, standing before an empty star monument, I can only hope that God in his grace will take me to the attic to liberate Sara's little gray rolls. Or strand me when need be . . . this side of the Promised Land.

15

seedstone ~ healing

I sit another Sunday in our log cabin church and brush my feet across its floor-
boards. The fawn-brown strips are worn from decades of hopeful congregants
come to worship, come to find their way. Outside, the maples thread their leaves
across a blue sky—now giving slack, now reining in the thousand joyful kites
that whistle and dip. I envy their delight, bent as I am beneath a past that weighs
on me like stone, making me unfeeling, sometimes cold with rage. Bury me in the
earth, I think, and the world will be a better place. I look down, forget the
maples, sink toward the floor. Then without warning a vision knocks, picks at
my elbows, lifts me past despair and pity. In my mind's eye a stone appears, the
unlikely birthplace of life. From its center, a brilliant wildflower rises. This pic-
ture is a promise of impossible healing. I inhale the moment and sing.

Garbage-picking is not a crime. If I want to sift through my neighbor's garbage, I am free to do so. I learned about this great American freedom because I read the story of A. J. Weberman in a book
called *Garbage Land*. Weberman liked to develop a truer understand-

ing of famous people by looking through their trash. When he was caught rifling through Bob Dylan's, a judge declared him innocent of illegal activity.

What sobered me was how Weberman's efforts sometimes highlighted people's guilt. On looking in Bella Abzug's trash, for instance, he found receipts for stocks in weapons-making companies. This would not be that unusual except that Bella Abzug was an antiwar activist.

When I read about this I felt sorry for Abzug. It must have been embarrassing to be exposed by some moldy strips of paper swimming around in smashed peas. As I considered her dilemma, though, I slipped into the shadows. If Weberman searched through my trash, what would he find? Or, if he searched the crumpled moments of my day, who would he really see?

Like Abzug, I stand for good causes. As a Christian I promote compassion for the lowly. But also like Abzug, I harbor warlike secrets. When I face someone in my intimate circle who exhibits weakness, I often seethe. With my spouse this can turn into accusation and blame; I once berated him for tripping on the sidewalk, as if he could have prevented it. I've also struggled against thoughts of slapping my children out of their neediness. Indeed, when she was little, I once slapped my eldest daughter across the face to stop her from crying. I was horrified by my behavior. Of course, she only cried harder.

My sister has faced similar feelings. We've discussed, with confusion and sadness, our tendency to become hard of heart in the face of weakness. We have wondered together whether our childhood years as survivors permanently scarred us, driving us to reject our loved ones in their moments of weakness.

At times I feel hopeless in the face of this question, believing that nothing can change me. My frailties seem so deep, so encompassing that I simply want to call it quits, forget about serving my family or the church.

In this regard I often identify with Moses. He was a gifted man who had the power of God right within reach. But Moses ruined his first real job by flying into a rage and killing an Egyptian rather than finding a way to justice. Understandably, he felt unfit and afraid, so he escaped to a life of exile.

During Moses' exile he slipped into a different cultural clan, eclipsed himself from the world he'd known, as if this would cover his act of burying an Egyptian in the sand. At this time, Moses had a son. But he did not name him anything hopeful. Instead he named him Gershom, which means "lonely stranger." By all indications Moses was paralyzed by self-doubt and a sense of ill-fittedness. In the end he was set back about forty years, making him the world's premier late-bloomer.

Though the situation was not so great for Moses, I like this about him. I identify with his late blooming. I also like the context of his blossoming moment. After forty years of retreat, God finally meets him on Horeb, the mountain whose name means "desert" or "desolation." After countless years of despair, God comes to Moses right where he stands: in the middle of barren ground. It's in this lifeless place that God's power erupts into Moses' life, promising a different future, a revision of the past.

But Moses is at risk of missing the moment; he's felt unfit for so long. I suspect this might be one reason God appeared as a burning bush. God had some extensive burning to do for Moses—burning of his doubts and fears and regrets.

I like to think that as God flamed into the path, he recited a poem by Madeleine L'Engle. I know there's no evidence to support this, but it would have been handy . . .

> My son goes down in the orchard to incinerate
> Burning the day's trash, the accumulation
> Of old letters, empty toilet-paper rolls, a paper plate,
> Marketing lists, a discarded manuscript, on occasion
> Used cartons of bird seed, dog biscuit.
> The fire rises and sinks; he stirs the ashes till the
>   flames expire.
> Burn, too, old sins, bedraggled virtues, tarnished
> Dreams, remembered unrealities, the gross
> Should-haves, would-haves, the unvarnished
> Errors of the day, burn, burn the loss
> Of intentions, recurring failures, turn
> Them all to ash.
> Incinerate the dross.
> Burn. Burn.

The day I sat in church scuffing the floorboards and saw that blossoming stone, I felt like God was a faithful Son at work in the orchard, incinerating the scraps of my bedraggled virtues, gross should-haves, errors of the day, recurring failures. The flame of the wildflower rising from stone was my burning bush, sent to say, "I will use you, damaged as you are."

How hopeful. It reminds me of Makoto Fujimura's discussion of an art installation at the Jewish Museum in New York. Commenting on a row of boulders in which an artist had planted seedlings, Fujimura said, "We need more creative visionaries who would dare even to plant seedlings in stone that will mature into trees." God is that creative visionary who does what is even more unimaginable. He uses the stone not as a planter but as a seed itself.

There's a wonderful children's book called *The Tin Forest* that captures this unique talent of God's—his vision and ability to take what is desolate and grow life from its entrails. In the story an old man lives "in a wide windswept place, near nowhere and close to forgotten, filled with all the things that no one wanted." His small house looks out "on other people's garbage and bad weather." Eventually he gets the idea to construct a forest. "Under the old man's hand, a forest emerged. A forest made of garbage. A forest made of tin." Time passes and animals come to the forest. Seeds grow. A real forest springs up. The story ends, "There once was a forest, near nowhere and close to forgotten, that was filled with all the things that everyone wanted."

God is like that old man. Under his hand a forest can emerge from the garbage of failure and want. From his fingers life can chatter into existence out of inert material. Sometimes the growth is shockingly immediate—the miracle of "stand up, take your mat and walk." But more often the miracle of rejuvenation takes time.

I think of the road to Siloam, walked by a man who was blind from birth (John 9). This man knew the pain of stepping on sharp objects, the embarrassment of hurting others accidentally, the shame of being called names, the isolation of exclusion. It was years before he met the moment of his healing, and even then the process was fraught with difficulty, fear and ambiguity. His journey was uneasy with no predictable end.

Jesus comes along with a promise of healing. But look how it goes. Jesus breathes into his space, spits and pushes the dirt, calls himself the Light of the World. He slathers mud on the beggar's eyelids, and the blind man wonders if this is the meaning of light, a strange combination of love and the spread of discomfort. Then Jesus breaks into his thoughts with an odd command: "Go, . . . wash in the Pool of Siloam" (John 9:7).

This pool is on the south side of the city, surely outside the acceptable Sabbath walking distance. How will the blind man find it, and should he really go? I imagine he thinks to ask Jesus, but already the Rabbi's voice is receding, garbled with the chirping sounds of the crowd.

Siloam means "sent," and now the blind man must feel the terror of going alone, without the healer who's spun him like a top, sent him careening into the day. The sun beats down. Dust tickles his nose. The mud cracks on his eyelids. Wandering down long paths, through narrow streets, past derisive whispers, he doubts and falters, asking in darkness, "Where is the Pool of Siloam?" Hours later someone tells him it's only one more corner. He circles into the open, but now, even so close, bumps on a jagged cobble, falls and finally crawls to the edge of the pool. By faith he slides his hand into the water, washes, not even knowing what healing will finally look like.

Sometimes I feel like this blind man. I don't know how and when healing will come, and I'm uncomfortable along the hard way—even though I know God has ordained the rise of a seedling

from stone, just as he ordained vision with a slather of mud. Yet I
have a comfort the blind man did not: a community of believers
among whom I sit Sunday after Sunday, where the tale of healing's
price is cradled and retold. I have a sister who still helps me untangle the pieces of our childhood by sharing memories and honest
reflections. And I have the Holy Spirit, who does not berate me
but welcomes me with truth and grace in my neediness.

16

sugar face ~ forgiveness

It is a sunny day over the river, perfect for a drive to the local museum. So the children and I pack into our wintergreen hatchback and go to Katonah. I pay a small fee to enter the dim silence, where we see a man we gaze at face to face. He seems to be made of fine stone, perhaps marble fashioned at the hands of a modern Michelangelo, destined to sit here forever with his broad nose, strong chin, steady eyes. We look at his lashes, read the wall card to the right. Media: burnt sugar. Turning to survey his cheeks, we see what we'd not seen before. Disintegration. This man, like it or not, is bowing to a humidity that will slowly eat away each feature, turn him into sweet nothing. His name none of us remember anymore. In our house we just call him Sugar Face.

Sometimes my spouse and I get into senseless fights. Like the night we squabbled over Rid-X. It is a biofriendly drain declogger, but it caused a good deal of unfriendliness between us for a while—until I sheepishly remembered that I had volleyed the first hurtful words. Recognizing my frailty, my status as a finite sugar face, I went upstairs and quietly said, "I'm sorry. I love you more than Rid-X."

I wish forgiveness and reconciliation were always this easy.

When my father's father died, I went to see the body. I had never been to such a small gathering of its kind. It was clear to me that the six people who made an appearance sat in a wake of unforgiveness. It lapped at our toes, pushed us like so much flotsam to the edge of the viewing room. There was not much to say.

My father was the only one among his brothers who showed up. He did it to honor his father, who'd left him a one-dollar inheritance. In fact, my grandfather left one dollar to each of his sons except the youngest, son of a second wife. The youngest received a full inheritance. My father did not hold this against my grandfather, at least not enough to abandon him at his death.

I think my father realized that this behavior from my grandfather was just more of the same anger and manipulation that had always plagued their relationship. And he refused to return the volley. He had slowly been admitting the truth—his dad was a furious man, condemning and degrading. But my father had begun to forgive him nonetheless.

This was expressed most poignantly to me in a poem my dad wrote a few years after my grandfather died. Not only did its verses recognize my grandfather's frailties, they also admitted something surprising. My own father had been reluctant to embrace the roles of husband and father that my grandfather so inadequately embodied. In fact, some of the ways my father treated women and children were geared toward proving himself to the man who never gave him a living inheritance of love.

I'm glad my father shared that poem with me. Seeing his pain and struggle with his own father was the beginning of my deeper forgiveness of him.

There was a time, after all, when I could not talk to my father on the phone without thinking, *I hate you, I hate you, I hate you.* When he'd end the conversation with "I love you," I would just say, "Thanks." I was angry with him about my whole life—a life haunted by a cruel stepfather, a life that felt fatherless, a life that lost several mothers because of his infidelities. I was grateful when he opened his heart to me and I could release my anger, grain by grain, to the wind.

It's convenient when forgiveness happens this way. Someone opens a door, invites us inside, lets us look at the cobwebbed corners the way my father let me. In fact, I always wish this had happened with my grandmother—the one who gardened her land with such great resolve.

Yet Grandma didn't change or reveal. The resolve and no-nonsense approach that made her so gifted, so dedicated to caring for her land and family, had a flip side. She felt no qualms about criticizing me with unchecked matter-of-factness. These criticisims hurt me in a way she probably never knew. Once, I told her to stop talking to me the way she did, but she simply repeated her criticism in different words, as if I'd asked her to explain herself more clearly. I boiled with anger; I did not want to hear in more detail how ugly I looked with my hair styled the way my mother used to style it. These words represented all the others I'd listened to over the years. Words about how she loved my father's first wife best. Words that painted my mother and my beloved stepmother Beezie as imposters. Words of favoritism about her first and loveliest granddaughter—a girl I never knew until adulthood.

One day, standing in my study, I was totally immersed in unforgiveness; I was thinking of my grandmother, savoring my bitterness. Suddenly, and quite uninvited, these questions rolled into my mind: "What if the people whose love you cherish held you to the standard to which you hold her? What if your loved ones only saw your faults, of which you have many? What is your unforgiveness but an idol set on a pedestal—the idol of you set in perfection against others?"

Unforgiveness as idolatry. I was stunned. But it made sense.

Before this moment, idolatry was one of those words I'd never related to. It belonged to those ancient people whom Jeremiah mocked when he said, "They say to wood, 'You are my father,' / and to stone, 'You gave me birth'" (Jeremiah 2:27). Or idolatry belonged to the people whose shrines I'd seen smothered with flower petals along the roadside in India. I was not an idolater, ever.

But after the string of questions assailed me in my study, I saw things differently. I read Romans 1 and noticed myself in it. Paul reminded me that those who worship and serve creatures instead of the Creator are heartless, filled with malice. And I was certainly filled with malice toward my grandmother. I was being heartless. I had essentially worshiped myself—a creature—by sitting on a self-righteous pedestal from which I could see my grandmother's failures but not my own.

I also considered that ancient peoples "inspired" their idols through a series of rituals meant to bring them to life. After this the worshipers treated the idol royally, dressing it in kingly robes.

They carried it in a regal parade and gave it fine foods. In my unforgiveness I certainly managed to treat myself royally, feeding myself the pure intentions and beautiful heart I denied my grandmother because of her hurtful actions.

More than this, the term *idol* can simply mean "a falsehood," and that also applies here. There is, after all, something exceedingly false in attributing all the goodness to myself and all the failure to another.

God has a lot to say about idols all through the Bible. And none of it is good news. "When you cry out for help, / let your collection of idols save you!" he says. "The wind will carry all of them off, / a mere breath will blow them away" (Isaiah 57:13). These words are forbidding. They poke me to attention and remind me that I must not bend to the temptation to be unforgiving. For if I bend, I am worshiping the idol of myself—one that does not have the power to face the wind.

I find this compelling, yet forgiveness is still a mountain to climb. Hand over hand I face disappointment. I need to mourn, like my father who slowly faced the truth of his father but did not turn away. Mostly I must come to terms with the discovery that someone I hoped in isn't marble after all, but just another cast of burnt sugar—a sweet nothing like me.

Living in the fragility of this discovery, I reframe the old adage about glass houses and stones. I tell myself, people with sugar faces shouldn't rain judgment. For God knows, as do my friends, my spouse and my children: I need forgiveness. I need grace too.

17

Lava rock ~ witness

Walking beneath dense clusters of maple and oak, I smile at our attempt to go on a family hike. We cannot move more than three feet before one of our girls plants herself on the trail. I use the opportunity to examine orange umbrella mushrooms, or drink from a metal thermos, or gaze upward at the lace of branches overhead. The girls push tiny fingers into dirt, search for buried treasure. Grey sparkle rocks and black obsidian, garnet-flecked beauties and common quartz. The earth bubbles with secrets waiting for someone to fumble them to light. "I used to collect rocks too," I tell my children, even as I hesitate to add another of their must-haves to our pack.

Back home I show them my geode—a gift my mother bought many years ago at an incense-filled Catholic cathedral. I reveal the outside first, let them touch the bland, bumpy surface. Then I turn the rock over. Blue crystal gems shine. And my children smile.

A curious thing happens when you forgive someone. Suddenly it is possible to tell that person things you couldn't say before. At least this is what happened between my father and me. After I began the process of forgiveness, I could deal with him as a whole person, the bumpy sides and the gems.

I could tell him, for instance, how disappointed I was when he made promises and didn't keep them. I could tell him that, from my perspective, the reason he broke those promises was that he constantly needed to be a savior. He'd make promises to me, and then he'd move on to the next person he could make promises to. It was good for his warm intentions of saving the world, but it was bad for our relationship.

I wrote him a letter that said, "This has got to change if we're going to continue to have a relationship. I can't live like this." I also described what it felt like—as if I were a drowning person he'd toss a lifesaver to only to neglect to pull me aboard. When he got the letter he called immediately, and we talked and cried. I admitted that I have the same issue—I want to save others. It makes me feel important.

In my faith life this has meant wanting to be like a Billy Graham or a Paul of Tarsus, which I clearly am not. For a long time I could not accept this. These men are Christian icons who've brought souls to Christ like industrial magnets. I, on the other hand, have always been lost in the volcano. Nobody that I know of has come to Christ through me.

I used to feel guilty about this, the way I felt guilty about selling a single stuffed animal for a fundraiser while my friend sold a hundred. But I'm thinking differently now, letting the guilt slip away. It's not like I never talk to people about God. In fact, I'm probably bothersome at times. Someone can be discussing French toast and I automatically see an amazing connection to God. So I say it.

More often than not, the person I'm speaking to kindly smiles at me like I'm a door-to-door peddler selling Amway. And we go our separate ways.

So I talk about God, but I don't see fruit in the form of conversions. Ironically, it is Paul who frees me from guilt. In I Corinthians 3 he is trying to settle a dispute about who is more important, himself or Apollos. And he says, "What, after all, is Apollos? And what is Paul? Only servants, through whom you came to believe—as the Lord has assigned to each his task. I planted the seed, Apollos watered it, but God made it grow" (I Corinthians 3:5-6).

Taking this to heart is a form of trust—that God will work when I least expect it, that despite my bland, bumpy exterior, he will unveil the shining hope within me to people with whom I share his words. And when the time is right, he'll send someone else to cultivate and harvest the spiritual fruit. It will happen, even if I'm not there to see it.

Somehow this reminds me of a scene from the novel *Gilead*. An elderly pastor looks out the window to see his wife and boy blowing bubbles to the cat. He writes to his son,

> I saw a bubble float past my window, fat and wobbly and ripening toward that dragonfly blue they turn just before they burst. So I looked down at the yard and there you were, you and your mother, blowing bubbles at the cat, such a barrage of them that the poor beast was beside herself at the glut of opportunity. . . . Some of the bubbles drifted up through the branches, even above the trees. You . . . were too intent on the cat to see the celestial consequences of your worldly endeavors.

Maybe there had been times when the son tried to persuade his father to come play with bubbles. Maybe that's why the son was out there with his mother—because he'd never been able to convince his father of the beauty of the activity. Maybe not. In any case it was finally a moment invisible to the son that captured the old man's heart. The son did not get to share his father's sudden joy at the discovery of bubble loveliness.

I like to remember this when I reflect that I've never shared the moment of bubbly God-discovery with anyone. I also like to remember Nebuchadnezzar. This Babylonian king was exceptionally involved with false gods, magicians, enchanters, sorcerers and diviners—all the kinds of people who couldn't point him to the Shining One.

When these people couldn't help him through a hard time, a season of night terrors, he called for Daniel. He had done this before to help him through a different hard time, but it only resulted in this: "Then King Nebuchadnezzar fell prostrate before Daniel and paid him honor and ordered that an offering and incense be presented to him" (Daniel 2:46). Not exactly the spiritual results Daniel was looking for, I'm sure.

Worse yet, before he called Daniel to solve his current problem, Nebuchadnezzar had tried to destroy Daniel's friends in a fiery furnace for refusing to worship his gods and a golden statue of himself. I wonder what hope Daniel had when he came before this king, interpreted his dream and said, "Let my advice be acceptable to you; break off your sins by being righteous, and your iniquities by showing mercy" (Daniel 4:27 NKJV).

One year later the king went insane, going out to the fields and eating grass like an ox. This went on for seven years, until his hair grew long as eagle feathers and his nails long as bird claws. In the end Nebuchadnezzar was alone, wet with dew, when he lifted his eyes to heaven and his reason returned. There in isolation he finally took Daniel's counsel, saying, "I praised the Most High; I honored and glorified him who lives forever" (Daniel 4:34). God brought forth the crowning spiritual fruit with Nebuchadnezzar, away from the crowds, in a way Daniel never could have.

For me, coming to maturity has meant accepting God's ability to bring people to spiritual ripeness without my final participation—or simply through others, like Billy Graham and Paul. In this way God does not indulge my need to be a savior. I'm only asked to play the child on a winding trail, stooping to fumble his hidden secrets into light . . . rarely knowing if someone will see them as a must-have.

18

cLImBINg ~ justIce

Sometimes when the sailboats and tugboats are finished traversing the river for the day, my friends pick past creeping juniper and white morning glories, ascend steep stone stairs to gather in this little house of mine. The chatter of children behind us, the door closed to a littered and crumbling street, we laugh our way into a sunset-yellow dining room. A small table is set with simple linens, brilliant colors of lemon, cobalt and red. There are rose china teacups, strawberries dipped in chocolate and orange-flecked scones, all provided by my husband's hospitality. It is comfort for an evening that will have its own discomforts. For we gather here with sobering books in hand to talk about the world, its deep needs and sorrows.

When I'm wrapped in my own chains, dwelling on the past and the injustices I've lived through, it's hard to get outside myself and help to change the world. Indeed, this state makes me vulnerable to what I call the "just is" syndrome. Focused on my own pain, my sense of vengeance or hopelessness, I look out at the rest of the world and say, well that's the way it *just is*.

On the other hand, when I am experiencing the freedom of healing, things change. I can begin to move from the "just is" view to the justice view of life. I can embrace the words of Toni Morrison: "The function of freedom is to free someone else." And I can invite a former enemy to join me in the endeavor.

As a place to begin, I started a group—a social issues book club where we would read about rain forest economies, modern-day slavery, inequities in education and so forth. I asked my friends to join. I asked my sister, who lives two hours away, to come. And I asked my father, who now lives below the Mason-Dixon line, to be a long-distance participant. He and I have never talked about much more than our hurts and apologies, so it's a good next step toward becoming true friends.

On this journey from "just is" to justice, with my father by my side, I feel like a child with fresh, wiggly toes. In his presence and before my own peers, I realize with some trepidation that I have choices. I can bind my wiggly toes like the ancient foot-binders did to preserve a delicate look. Or I can spread them out and start walking, even climbing the steep stairs of change.

Right now I'm choosing to climb. This hasn't been an easy decision in the face of objections from those who prefer delicacy in the Christian life and who find my choice brash. For instance, at least one person has openly questioned whether I'm even a Christian because I started the social issues reading club. On the other hand, people who know more and have done more about justice might find my small steps quaint or even fruitless. Again, at least one person criticized, saying I haven't "done much." In each case I'm comforted by those who've gone before me in the face of criticisms and unknowns.

I try to remember people like Karangathe, a worker in Kenya's green belt movement, who says,

> It's a long way to Nairobi . . . a very long way. I don't know how I'm going to get there, but I just start walking. And someone comes along who is going the same direction. Someone picks me up on a bicycle and takes me part of the way. I get off and walk. Then maybe in the next town I meet someone who picks me up and takes me a bit further. Then I walk some more. The most important thing is that I know where I want to go—and that I just keep walking.

Karangathe's experience encourages me. I don't have to know exactly how to get to justice-town, yet as a follower of Jesus I have to get up and move. Like anyone on a long journey, I shouldn't be surprised when the walk is full of rest stops and unexpected rides. And of course there will be naysayers who stand on the sides of the road.

Because it is a long way to Nairobi, I have to keep up hope. I have to trust that someday I will get there. In the meantime my walk begins here with the first steps. And the way I see it, the first steps involve asking questions. What are the problems in the world? What is fueling them? How do I become a problem-solver? Finally, and perhaps the most difficult, how am I a part of the problem?

This last question is foundational. And it is the question I learned to ask in a new way one night at our book club. We were talking about the Really Rich, and someone told a story about her town to illustrate how the rich guys are fueling the problems in our world.

In this town, a Really Rich guy built a house. He built it behind a big rock that spoiled the view. So he went to the town to get a permit to move the big rock, but the town denied him. Maybe the town was miffed that the guy was Really Rich or they had inside information about the rock—as in, maybe it was holding down that side of the community like a kid on the far side of a seesaw.

So the Really Rich guy accepted the town's decision to leave the land untouched. Then one night, an enormous flock of emperor penguins rolled the rock to Antarctica with their birdy feet—well, not exactly. The truth is, my friend exclaimed, "The rich guy moved the rock in the night! Can you believe the gall? How could he deface the community like that?"

I was the first to chime in, "How could he?" Then in the next moment, this little thought came. "Who or what do I deface in my community for the pleasure of the view?" The word *deface* stood out. De-face. As in, erase the face or ignore the face so I don't have to look into the eyes, watch the lips move, hear the cries or respond in compassion. Suddenly it was clearer than it had ever been. It is not just the rich and powerful who are sometimes corrupt. I can't just blame society or our big leaders. I too am responsible for defacing the world. How do I do it? And why am I not always compassionate or passionate to bring change?

To this, I like to consider a particular biblical moment. After Jesus had been with a crowd for three days, looking into their eyes, he told the disciples, "I have compassion for these people; they . . . have nothing to eat. If I send them home hungry, they will collapse on the way" (Mark 8:2-3).

Jesus, being God, would have compassion even if he hadn't been with the crowd three days, but that's not how the event is communicated. The writer mentions Jesus' extended involvement with the crowd. And I take this description as a gift—a bicycle ride on the way to Nairobi. It tells me that compassion can be related to extended proximity—though perhaps not physical as much as emotional proximity. Maybe, I consider, I am not compassionate because I feel removed from people and issues. Joining this simple book club has served as a way to get close, to cultivate compassion.

The next step, of course, is what to do about the stirring in my heart. This is not a simple step by any means. I see this by further exploring the scene of Jesus and his disciples with the crowd of hungry people. After Jesus expressed his compassion for the hungry crowd, his companions answered in classic disciple form, "But where in this remote place can anyone get enough bread to feed them?" (Mark 8:4).

I relate to this response. When my heart is stirred in compassion, I often feel too small or unmotivated to solve the problems in the desert. Yet as someone who is mature in faith, I'm called to be a problem-solver. Well, more than called. Shouted at.

It never ceases to surprise me how indelicate God can be when he wiggles his toes and walks. Sometimes he simply refuses to be bound by polite convention. In Isaiah he tells the prophet, "Shout it aloud, do not hold back. / Raise your voice like a trumpet" (Isaiah 58:1). In my house we do not allow this kind of boisterous behavior. But in the courts of God it seems to be a different story. So Isaiah shouts the Lord's words at the people:

> Is not this the kind of fasting I have chosen:
>   to loose the chains of injustice

and untie the cords of the yoke,
to set the oppressed free
and break every yoke?

Is it not to share your food with the hungry
and to provide the poor wanderer with shelter—
when you see the naked, to clothe him,
and not to turn away from your own flesh and blood?
(Isaiah 58:6-7)

Jesus revives this shout in a three-exclamation-point paragraph, where he says to the Pharisees, "You give a tenth . . . but you have neglected the more important matters of the law—justice, mercy and faithfulness" (Matthew 23:23).

Somehow with the spread of years all this shouting has come down to a whisper in certain circles. Paul Coughlin speculates about the change in volume: "Much of it stems from an inaccurate picture of Jesus. Contrary to the common fiction many churches promote of 'gentle Jesus, meek and mild,' Jesus was both amazingly compassionate and assertive. In the Gospel of Mark alone we see Jesus confronting people, healing people, yelling at people, calling people names."

Additionally, our hesitance to do the hard, assertive work of Jesus may be due to a lack of connection to Jewish thought. I have a friend who converted from Judaism to Christianity, and he's tried to explain to me the Jewish concept of a *tsaddiq*. The *tsaddiq* is a perfectly wise and righteous one; nobody can really claim the title except Messiah. My friend was astonished to see in Jesus the fulfillment of the traditional *tsaddiq* figure.

I was fascinated to see the root meaning of the Hebrew term: It

means "straightness" in the physical sense and has two main trans-
lations: "righteous" and "just." So Jesus, the awaited *tsaddiq*, is a
straight-on justice-incarnate person. This rather precludes the
meek and mild Jesus, because (to borrow a book title) justice is
conflict. Though the work of justice needn't be angry and rude,
some people will inevitably see it that way. The moneychangers in
the temple, for instance, probably thought Jesus' whip-thrashing in
the midst of their "fair market" was a bit indelicate.

This brings me back to the moral thumb-twiddling of the disciples in the desert, who stood by thinking they shouldn't solve the
crowd's hunger problem. I'm not saying they shied away from any
assertiveness required on their part. But they didn't consider taking
a bold step of faith even though they'd put their faith in a bold
Jesus. This is perhaps odd, seeing that God tells us we receive his
tsedaqah when we turn to him and are saved—which makes us little
Christs, little *tsaddiqim*, little straight-on justice-incarnates (see Isaiah 45:22, 24).

To live as a grace-bearing justice-incarnate who models bold
faith to my children and their generation, I discover I have to be
willing to use my power—even if it's only at first the power to take
my father's hand and climb toward Nairobi.

19

ROXABOXEN ~ HEAVEN

Night moves in across the river, descends on my town whose name means "stone upon stone." Mourning doves settle amid the hemlocks, spreading silence like a silken veil over the yard. Upstairs I open pages of delight, a story for our little ones, the way my own mother used to open stories and poetry for me. Tonight we read of Marian and a place called Roxaboxen, a place that seems eternal. To get to Roxaboxen the characters must ford an imaginary river, the River Rhode. In this pretend town are rocks and sand, boxes and prickly cactus, neighborhood children—those who come first and those who must have come after and those who must have come before, for "Roxaboxen had always been there and must have belonged to others." The children of the story grow up and tell of the place to their own children. More than fifty years later one character goes back to find that Roxaboxen is still there. "She could see the white stones bordering Main Street, and there where she had built her house the desert glass still glowed—amethyst, amber, and sea green."

I like stories that broach the subject of eternity, whether they're children's stories or serious grown-up stories like the one in the film *Wit*, directed by Mike Nichols. In that film an aged professor comes to visit her dying student Vivian, whose mind flashes back to a conversation the two had long ago. "Nothing but a breath, a comma, separates life from life everlasting," the professor had scolded her, because Vivian had used an unscholarly Donne edition to explore the poem "Death Be Not Proud." The unscholarly text, the professor emphasized, had the audacity to use a semicolon instead of a comma in the last line, thus making the barrier between life, death and eternal life seem insuperable.

The professor's comment makes it seem as if our move from life to death should be like an IRA rollover—a short transaction from one account to another, seamless to the client. There is perhaps some truth to this. Yet I've witnessed too many dying souls and noted the striking presence of the semicolon, the human tendency to hang on to life's full sentence with tenacity and great pause before moving on. In at least four cases, I remember that someone had to give the go-ahead to the dying person. "It's okay; let go. You can go home now." And with this permission, the dying person tiptoed off his last punctuated pause into the full sentence of the great unknown, to the other side of the river.

My aunt, who sat by my mother and watched my Grammy die, put it this way: "I always thought that death was like what you see in the movies—peaceful—but it's not. Death is a struggle. Gram tried her best not to die. Her whole body fought the inevitable."

And yet.

Henri Nouwen, considering Rembrandt's prodigal son painting, says, "It had brought me into touch with something within me . . . that represents the ongoing yearning of the human spirit, the yearning for a final return, an unambiguous sense of safety, a lasting home." Nouwen expresses what the writer of Hebrews attributes to the faithful of the past: "They admitted that they were aliens and strangers on earth . . . looking for a country of their own. . . . They were longing for a better country—a heavenly one" (Hebrews 11:13-14, 16).

Or we are, for those who prefer the words of Annie Dillard, sojourners. "It doesn't seem to be here that we belong, here where space is curved, earth is round. . . . It is strange here, not quite warm enough, or too warm, too leafy, or inedible, or windy, or dead. It is not, frankly, the sort of home for people one would have thought of—although I lack the fancy to imagine another."

Maybe it is our lack of ability to imagine another home that keeps us poised on the semicolon like a timid high-diver, unwilling to flip away from the only home we've known—earth and the touch of our loved ones. This is not necessarily a bad thing. If we had too much imagination for the future we might start diving into the water headlong before our time. Then who would be left to help new children come to Roxaboxen to play? Somebody has got to stay by the River Rhode before crossing the River Styx. That is just how it needs to be.

So there's this needful tension on either side of the semicolon (or the comma, depending on your preference in Donne editions). In life we have a vague desire to ford our way home to heaven. But we have much to do before touching our toes to the water. There are boxes to set up as houses, pebbles to exchange with newfound friends and desert glass to arrange in the bright rays of the sun.

It's a relief for me to think this way. After all, the last thing I want to face when I'm dying is a sense of guilt. There should be some freedom to say, "You know, I really don't want to do this. I'm stuck on the semicolon because I like my job here. I still want to place little white stone on little white stone at the edges of the streets." In other words, I don't want to have to pretend that just because I'm a Christian I'm ready to dive. Some people expect this readiness from us. Yet the Bible, in its lack of details about heaven, which is perhaps simply a redeemed earth, hardly inspires such readiness.

On the other hand, some people don't ever want us to be ready to go. They hang back from giving permission to die. I understand this is due to both love and the lack of imagination Annie Dillard expresses. At the same time, I hope the people who stand by my bed (if it happens that way) will find the courage to speak truth, reminding me there's grace beyond the semicolon. I want them to admit that I'm really moving on, that my time has come, that God is not by some miracle going to keep me playing in the desert any longer.

Not knowing what some of my friends wanted when they were dying, I hung back, afraid to comfort them with truth. I sat by their bedsides wanting to read these words of Jesus from John 14: "Do not let your hearts be troubled. . . . In my Father's house are many rooms; if it were not so, I would have told you. I am going there to prepare a place for you. And if I go and prepare a place for you, I will come back and take you to be with me that you also may be where I am" (John 14:1-3).

In the movie *Wit*, when the professor comes to comfort Vivian on her deathbed, she offers to recite some Donne, but Vivian gasps a quiet "No." So in the end, the professor pulls a children's book from her bag; it's a gift she's taking to her great-grandson. From the pages of *The Runaway Bunny*, she reads,

Once there was a little bunny who wanted to run away. So he said to his mother, "I am running away."

"If you run away," said his mother, "I will run after you. For you are my little bunny."

"If you run after me," said the little bunny, "I will become a fish in a trout stream and I will swim away from you."

"If you become a fish in a trout stream," said his mother, "I will become a fisherman and I will fish for you."

Finally, later in the story, the little bunny says he will become a bird, and the mother says, "If you become a bird and fly away from me . . . I will be a tree that you come home to."

Though this story is not quite John 14, it expresses to me the parental love of Jesus: "I will fish for you, I will be a tree that you come home to, I will come again and take you to myself."

There is some comfort in knowing that Jesus stands on the other side waiting to embrace me more fully than I've ever known—that, indeed, he will cast his line for me with a fatherly love that surpasses the imperfect love of my own father. And that, with a motherly love that surpasses the imperfect love of my own mother, he's arranging a home for me with a fire at the hearth and warm bread on the table.

Therefore my heart is glad and my tongue rejoices;

my body also will rest secure,

because you will not abandon me to the grave,
   nor will you let your Holy One see decay.

You have made known to me the path of life;
   you will fill me with joy in your presence,
   with eternal pleasures at your right hand. (Psalm 16:9-11)

Sometimes I wonder about these pleasures. I wonder about my new home, where my body will rest secure. I consider that Jesus has promised, in the tradition of a marriage custom that lasted well into the last century, to prepare a place for me just as a groom prepared a new home for his bride.

We see this kind of preparation in a Laura Ingalls Wilder book, wherein Laura describes how Almanzo prepares a new home for her through the work of his hands. On their marriage day he brings her to the door and quietly goes to do chores while she explores the house. There are neatly plastered walls, large windows, a wide bed and a pantry with numerous shelves and drawers.

But this is not all. The house is also veiled with the familiar—silken remnants of her previous life. Ma's red-checked cloth graces the table. Laura's dove quilt is spread on the bed. Her trunk, filled with belongings, stands against the wall.

First Corinthians 3 suggests that our works, whether straw or gold, follow us to heaven, much like Laura's past turned up in her new home. Revelation puts it this way:

"Blessed are the dead who die in the Lord from now on."
   "Yes," says the Spirit, "They will rest from their labor, for

their deeds will follow them." (Revelation 14:13)

Thinking of this, I'm almost willing to trade my semicolon for a comma, to let there be but a breath between life and life everlasting. At night when I tuck my children into bed and remember that they'll eventually go on without me, I'm almost willing to someday leave them. To accept that they'll continue a portion of the play I began. And I take comfort that the very desert glass I arrange beside them now will someday glow in my home with Jesus—amethyst, amber and sea green.

20

bLood from a stone ~ compLetion

Far from my river on the shores of a lake, my grandmother waits for someone to ease her from her chair. This is the woman who farmed ten acres single-handedly, who lined her shelves with currant jams and sweet pickles, who built train sets and dollhouses and brought them to life with lights and sound, who faithfully knelt by my childhood bedside and taught me to pray, "Now, I lay me down to sleep, I pray the Lord my soul to keep." Blind and deaf, she thinks she is worthless. The beliefs of the world have settled themselves squarely on her heart. (You are useless, old—a dry and bloodless stone.) Somehow she has forgotten or we have forgotten that even songbirds murmur till the sun goes down beyond the cliffs.

In our culture, when someone turns forty, or even thirty, we joke that he is "over the hill." We celebrate the occasion with black balloons, gag gifts like adult diapers and high-fiber drinks, and tongue-in-cheek condolences. It's all in fun. And I admit I've been an enthusiastic participant at times.

Yet I remember what someone said to me long ago: whenever we make light of something we betray a deeper belief. Looking at the middle-year birthday parties of America, it doesn't take much to discern our hidden belief: we Americans think of aging as a downhill ride.

No wonder, as Ellen Langer points out, we "rarely [use] the term *development* . . . to describe changes in the later years." Development, of course, implies some kind of growth. Aging, on the other hand—well, that means black balloons slowly deflating into the corners of the house.

This is not to suggest that growing older doesn't have its challenges; every age surely does. But I think Langer is on to something. In her book *Mindfulness* she includes a chapter called "Mindful Aging" that highlights eye-opening research. After reading her findings, I will think twice about giving a thirty-year-old black balloons or telling an elder to "just sit down" so she doesn't tire herself out.

What Langer found in study after study was that "old" is too often a state of mind, not a state of fact—even in people aged eighty and up. In a series of studies that raised the bar for elderly participants, she and her colleagues saw dramatic results—from memory loss reversal to prolonged life, improved hearing and vision, increased emotional satisfaction, renewed hand strength, and so on.

Langer concludes, "Most of the arbitrary limits we set on our development in later life are not based on scientific information at all. Our own mental picture of age, based on hundreds of small premature cognitive commitments, will shape the life we lead in our own late adulthood." Bring on the yellow balloons. Grandma, get up and dance.

I say this lightly, but there's a serious call: it may be time for the church to encourage the thought that growing old is a vital opportunity for new or deepened spiritual tasks. Because teaching that focuses simply on care for the aged could promote the feebleness that Langer saw reversed.

This need for visionary teaching on the spiritual work of the aged struck me even before I read Langer. It bowled me over when my gardening grandma told me in her later years that she didn't want me to see her because she felt so useless. With sorrow, I wrote her a letter. "I need to see you," I told her. "You give me hope for my future, that God can carry me through until I see him." Then I said, "Even though you can no longer see or hear, knit or garden, I thank you for the way your love still knits me together and nurtures my family whenever you pray."

In my church there has been some modeling of this vision—that those in their later years can lead vital, if redirected, ministries. We have several who minister in prayer, some who take time to visit the sick, one who started a nursing home ministry when he was eighty-eight (where he preached with fervor until he died) and another who invited people into her home even when she was no longer mobile and was approaching death. It is pure delight to have seen these elders living with great expectations.

God himself seems to have great expectations for the older generation. Joel says, "I will pour out my Spirit on all people. / . . . Your old men will dream dreams" (Joel 2:28). It makes me wonder what God might be wishing to tell us through the elders among us.

What dreams and visions, what wisdom might he want to pour out? If only we younger ones opened our hands for it, if only more of our elders expected such visitation.

In Luke we find two older people who keenly expected visitation—Simeon and Anna. Simeon, one assumes, is advanced in years, as he's waiting to see Messiah before he dies (see Luke 2:25-35). And it's fitting that Simeon means "God hears." Who knows how well Simeon himself could hear anymore? Yet at a time of life when this faculty begins to fail, he was still filled with a spirit of sensitivity to bright songs of revelation. Regardless of his physical condition, he could hear inwardly the One who never stops hearing and can get around our frailties. Indeed, Luke tells us that the Holy Spirit was speaking to Simeon, revealing that he would see Messiah before his death. Then, at the precise time, Simeon heard the Lord urging him to the temple, where he witnessed the new child come to bring salvation.

Meeting Jesus' family, Simeon played a special role. He prophesied about their future, he praised God for their present, and he blessed them so they would someday remember this moment and rejoice that God had been with them from the start.

It's good for parents to help mold an appropriate vision for their children's future. How doubly powerful this would be if it also came from the previous generation—grandparents and elder church members who'd play more than Santa Claus and take on the prophetic role of a Simeon, saying, "This is the kind of person I see God has fashioned you to be."

Similarly, in a society where too many of us suffer from a bewildering sense of aimlessness, what a vibrant task it could be for our elders to reassure us with their praises to God for our lives, the way Simeon praised God for the life of Jesus. These praises could be a beautiful form of offering—just one way that mature people could shepherd others who are still early in their journeys. I like the way Bill McConnell expresses such offerings in his poem "Community Life."

> Old trees, hospitable as small towns
> no longer afraid that high water, fire
> or some endemic blight
> will shrivel early growth
> but now satisfied
> that more summers and winters
> will not dislodge them,
> bear offerings—
> landmarks, reference points, sanctuary—
> to hearten pilgrims
> whose songs still tremble, newborn.

In my in-laws' culture, the elderly play this role every time you see them. Even if they can't stand on their own two feet, they beckon you into their space. I can remember more than one occasion when, like a Simeon in the temple, some older person has put a hand over my head to bless me. Through those fingertips I've felt the warm sap of love and encouragement that says, "Keep on. You've got a journey to fulfill."

When I look at Anna, who's also at the temple when Jesus is presented, I see she fills a similar role to that of Simeon. A widow of about one hundred years old, she's lived without a husband for eighty-four years. There is no mention of children, which seems to fit the description of her life—that is, "She never left the temple but worshiped night and day, fasting and praying" (Luke 2:37). Anna, like Simeon, praises God for Jesus' life. She too hears God's revelation, and then, like a morning bird, she spreads the news to anyone who has ears to hear. In all, she models an impressive late career change—from monastic to itinerant preacher.

I like that Anna's name means "grace." For she is full of this special quality. At a hundred years strong, having been alone for a lifetime, facing the humility of age, she could have easily been filled with bitterness. But she is vibrant with the color of hope and enthusiasm, maintaining an eye toward redemption.

Compare Anna to the old man we meet in Ecclesiastes. Whereas Anna reaches for redemption and continues to develop, he increasingly moves toward a habit of consumption and self-centeredness. Looking back on his life, he says pessimistically, "For dreams come with many cares. . . . The lover of money will not be satisfied with money" (Ecclesiastes 5:3, 10 NRSV).

How could he know this? If the man is Solomon, as some tradition holds, we see that he idolized the very abundance God freely promised him in his youth. For Solomon collected twenty-five tons of gold annually. He amassed thousands of horses. He made treaties that preserved and enhanced his wealth, and these treaties were often sealed with a gift of women. Indeed he boasted seven hundred wives and three hundred concubines.

The writer of 1 Kings suggests that Solomon crossed a line he should not have (see 1 Kings 11). And in Deuteronomy 17:16-17, we see that a king should not "acquire great numbers of horses for himself" or "accumulate large amounts of silver and gold."

In the end, even though Solomon commissioned the house of God, a redemptive structure built with massive stones, this did not shelter him from despair. In disillusionment he concluded, "Whoever quarries stones will be hurt by them" (Ecclesiastes 10:9 NRSV; see also I Kings 5:17). So he entered old age in poverty of spirit. Even worse, the biblical storyteller dismantles Solomon's glory in one fell swoop: "And his heart was not fully devoted to the LORD his God, as the heart of David his father had been" (I Kings 11:4). As if to mirror this dismantled glory, his kingdom fell apart after his death.

I know that my American culture, even my Christian culture, tends to seek a life that is more like Solomon's and less like Anna's and Simeon's, focusing on consumption more than redemption. As Darrell L. Bock says, our contentment is "based on externals that slowly wither away." Conversely, the psalmist sets a redemptive vision before us. Rather than rooting ourselves in things that fade, we can be like a "tree planted by streams of water, / which yields its fruit in season / and whose leaf does not wither" (Psalm 1:3). "They will still bear fruit in old age, / they will stay fresh and green, proclaiming, 'The LORD is upright'" (Psalm 92:14-15).

I want to be like this tree, in which the birds of the air make a home. I want to offer shade and fruit. I want to be full of life and grace, for my family and the world. So I ask my elders to murmur the psalmist's vision as a prayer and a blessing for me—may I continue to live the adventure of stone crossings, but may I also take root by the stream . . . to show that the Lord is still upright. Even as I lay me down to sleep.

epilogue

I live far from my grandmother and do not get to see her much. I
depend on my father, who cares for her, to give me news of her life.
The news has been difficult. My father tells me she has lapsed into
virtual speechlessness. Occasionally she will say a word. Mostly she
stares into space. Hearing these reports, I did not expect to ever be
blessed with another word from my grandmother. Yet I felt motivated to make another visit, if only to hug her and show my love
and gratitude for her life before she passes on. So this past summer
I flew south to see her, and this is what happened . . .

*We are at the dining room table. Plates and glasses clink. Children chatter, make
silly faces. Grandma, ever silent, sits to my right. Aunt Wilma, just as old but
more lucid, is shouting, "You're writing a book, aren't you? What's it called?"*

I shout back with my working title: "Secrets in Stone!"

*Aunt Wilma smiles, a twinkle in her eyes. My grandmother shifts in her
seat. "I had a stone," she says.*

All eyes turn to her. An entire sentence has fallen from her speechless mouth. Then the questions begin. "A stone? What stone? Where did you get it?" Her jaw is tense with effort and another miracle of speech flows out. "I gave it to him."

She is looking at my father, who in the ensuing silence finishes the story. "She picked up a stone somewhere in Germany when she was six years old. She had it for almost eighty years—carried it through the war, kept it through immigration, packed it safely through every move. About two years ago, she said it was time to give it to me. So she handed it over with a little note. I can show it to you later."

As he promised, my father showed me my grandmother's stone. It is dark gray with a large white eye spot, palm-sized, flat and silky smooth. I rubbed it on my face. I smelled it. I even licked it when no one was looking. My father declared that someday, when the time is right, he will pass it on to me along with the note from my grandmother:

I picked up this stone from a brook in Hannover-Döhren in Germany when I was about six years old. I have treasured it ever since. I hope that you will treasure it as well. Love, Mutti.

When I read the note my throat tightened. My grandmother freely gave her treasure to the next generation. Oddly, it struck me that my book on faith was like my grandmother's experience. For as she picked up her river stone so early in life only to pass it on, I picked up my faith stone when I was just a child. Like she, I decided that the time was right to give it over.

And so here it is, or was—the story, the vision, the challenge and comfort of my life's faith, a faith that has shown its grace in both the hard and hidden places. It is a gift to my children and to whoever deigns to be a spiritual child. Like my grandmother before me, I can only say,

I picked up this stone when I was about six years old. I have treasured it ever since. I hope that you will treasure it as well.

DISCUSSION QUESTIONS

Chapter I: Stepping Stones ~ conversion

1. Do you think conversion is a one-time event or a process? What are the implications either way?

2. What are the potential benefits and drawbacks of settling on a personal "conversion story"?

3. What aspects of the Christian story might seem like a "fairy tale"? Compare the Christian story to some other nonreligious historical events. Are these other events any less "fairy tale" in quality? Explain.

4. Respond to the story about Opal—how she almost bought the same house that the author's father and stepmother did, but then prayed room by room instead, later returning by chance to the same house in response to the piano-for-sale ad. What aspects of the story make it seem like coincidence? Or, conversely, like direct intervention by God?

5. What is it about conversion that can stir up anger in others? How might a new Christian handle this?

6. Consider some of your own hard experiences. How have they either drawn you to or repelled you from God?

7. Are there hidden places in your life that need healing? What

would it take for you to open these places to God's tender searching and grace?

Chapter 2: Christmas Coal ~ shame

1. How would you define "shame"? Try to describe the feelings that accompany it.

2. What part did shame play in the Adam and Eve story? How does shame function either positively or negatively in your life and in society in general?

3. Do you agree that if there were no God our actions wouldn't matter? Do you think we would still experience shame if God didn't exist?

4. Respond to the knowledge that Jesus took the full form of shame. Reflecting on his final earthly experiences, how is this evident? (Compare Matthew 26–27 to Psalm 22.)

5. Jesus calls himself a worm, or *towla*. Turn the image and turn it again. What does it bring to your heart and mind?

6. Is there any way that we, his servants, may also be called to assume the form of a towla? (See I Peter 4:8.)

7. Reflecting on your past, is there some shame that still holds you back in your emotions or actions? Explore how Jesus' gracious journey into shame might free you. Or consider why this might not make any difference.

Chapter 3: Tossed Treasure ~ messiness

1. If you discovered you could obtain a Cat in the Hat machine to

clean up the messes of life, would you want one? What challenges might arise in trying to use it? Does this reveal anything about the complexities of God's cleanup efforts in the world?

2. Do you agree that a life in Christ does not exempt us from messiness?

3. Consider the image of persistent hands untangling chains. Does this resonate with how God works to clean things up in your life? How have you been either seeking or sabotaging God's work to untangle your soul or certain situations?

4. Do you believe that God is acting in line with his grace in your life and the world? What helps you to believe this? What hinders?

5. If you woke up tomorrow and were arrested and evicted from your home, how would this affect your life? What kinds of feelings would you face? Challenges? Opportunities?

6. Priscilla became a refugee. In what ways did the various aspects of her life mirror this reality even before it was her reality? What aspects of your life are similar or different?

7. Priscilla showed grace of speech, hospitality and flexibility. What kinds of soul work help form these qualities in a person? Which area do you desire to work on right now?

8. Is there anything about Christ's grace toward you that can help you face the messiness of life with courage and generosity?

Chapter 4: Heron Road ~ suffering

1. This chapter distinguishes between a "Shiloah conversion" and

an "Assyria conversion." How would you describe the difference? Do you think that certain people are predisposed to a certain kind of conversion journey? Why or why not?

2. Do you think it's okay for God to use the "Assyria method" when this can undoubtedly cause severe suffering? How does this concept fit with the idea of a loving, compassionate God?

3. Read Isaiah 42:3. Does the work of Jesus fit with God's choice to let us hunger or suffer?

4. Why do some people seem immune to the hunger of life without God? Similarly, why do some people seem to have a comfortable life, without a hint of Assyria in sight—even though they are not seeking God? (Read Romans 1:20-32 for one viewpoint.)

5. If we choose to live as "wild grapes" or the "prodigal" (which Romans 3:10 suggests we all do to some extent), why might it make sense for God to retract his provision and protection? Do you think he ever completely retracts his provision and protection?

6. Whether we come by way of Shiloah or Assyria is ultimately not as important as the fact that we come. However, there may be advantages and disadvantages related to each of the paths. Explain what you think they may be.

7. Some people face their death in Assyria, never choosing the grace of God. Why do you believe anyone would make such a choice?

Chapter 5: Sword in the Stone ~ resistance

1. We can take two approaches to the devil and spiritual battle: ignore or deny the issues, or frank discussion. Why might some

prefer to ignore or deny? Are there any risks to engaging in frank discussion? Benefits?

2. The prayers of the people "from the little church" stopped the advance of the author's stepfather. He never bothered the family again. Do you think prayer is always this protective? Explain.

3. If the devil cannot ultimately stake our heads on the city walls, why do you think he bothers to hunt us?

4. What factors influence your belief, or disbelief, regarding the devil and spiritual battle?

5. Do any of the "proofs" of invisible spiritual realities discussed in this chapter resonate with you? Why or why not?

6. Do you feel you tend to "put on the full armor of God" or leave it in the closet? Are certain areas more of a struggle than others? What makes them so?

7. How do you think the different parts of the armor actually succeed in foiling the evil hunter?

8. What role might grace play in helping prepare you for spiritual battle?

Chapter 6: Howe's Cave ~ baptism

1. Have you ever been baptized? If so, describe your experience. If not, have you ever witnessed a baptism? Describe the details as you remember them.

2. What's the value of baptism, in your opinion? If you have been baptized, was it meaningful to you? Why or why not?

3. What would an ideal baptism look like if you could plan it out?

What kind of context would you choose, what kinds of rituals? For instance, do the ideas of celebrating a Passover, collecting memorial stones, or drinking milk and honey interest you?

4. In what ways do you understand water as "death"? As "life"? Do these understandings provide deeper meaning concerning baptism?

5. Is there any way in which baptism can play the role of dyeing one's life? In what way does baptism signal "no turning back"? What other kinds of physical signs and steps might someone take to signal new life?

6. How is Christian baptism similar to and different from rituals you know of in other religions? Does this strengthen or diminish baptism as a sign of grace for the Christian religion?

7. If you've already been baptized, what was your journey like after the experience? Did it empower you, or did you, like Jacob, enter a time of wrestling with God?

8. In what ways could the one-time event of baptism be an ongoing conduit of grace? Is this something to reach for? Why or why not?

Chapter 7: Palisade Cliffs ~ doubt

1. What is doubt?

2. Is it possible to have a faith free of doubt? Is it desirable?

3. If you meet someone who's doubting his faith, how might you handle his concerns?

4. Why do people sometimes keep doubts to themselves? Are

there dangers in doing so? Are there dangers in sharing our doubts?

5. What kinds of real things nudge you into doubting your faith? What kinds of equally real things about God pull you out of doubt?

6. Why do you think Jesus lets us experience moments of doubt? What criticisms might be leveled at him for doing so? Does the grace of Jesus help us meet our doubts?

Chapter 8: Holding Pfaltzgraff ~ inclusion

1. What does it mean to you to "live on the inside"?

2. Describe an experience in which you distinctly felt like an outsider. How did it feel? In your opinion, why were you perceived as an outsider by the "insiders"?

3. What kinds of dynamics encourage insider-outsider thinking? Do any of these dynamics make you potentially vulnerable to becoming an outsider? An insider?

4. Are there dangers to insider-outsider thinking? If so, what are they for the insider? For the outsider?

5. Discuss some reasons why people may think Christianity is exclusive. Do you agree or disagree with these reasons? Conversely, how is Christianity uniquely inclusive?

6. The movement of the tabernacle from heaven to the Israelites to Jesus to our bodies reversed our condition as outsiders (see I Corinthians 6:19). Is there any way you could use this movement as a metaphor or a map for "inside-out" growth in your own life?

7. Jesus' gracious act of opening his heart to outsiders came at great cost. What kinds of cost might you face if you open your heart to someone or to a group that has been your outsider? On the other hand, what are the potential benefits?

8. Do you believe there are eternal consequences for people who, after receiving God's open heart, patch it closed in their relationships with others? Conversely, do you believe there are eternal rewards for people who live with the gracious, open heart of God?

Chapter 9: Indiana Jones ~ fear

1. Do you agree that fear of death is a common human emotion? Why do you think some people are afraid to die?

2. Hebrews 2:15 says that Jesus has freed us from the fear of death. What might this mean, especially since a Christian may still express fear of dying? Are there different aspects of the fear of death?

3. Peacemaking is often viewed as a "soft" mission as opposed to the "hard" mission of war. Considering the story of Jonah, do you agree that peacemaking is a soft mission?

4. We are commanded to love our enemies in order to share the grace of the gospel. How prepared do you feel to live this out? Do you feel more like Jonah or Jesus?

5. Who represents your Nineveh? Your Tarshish? Do you feel any need to adjust your goals and efforts in light of this? What small steps can you take right now to do so?

6. The sailors decided to use a cultural tool—a form of "lots"—

to determine who was at fault for the storm. Seeing that Jonah got the winning stone, what does this suggest about the interplay of our cultural tools with God's activities?

7. Have you ever faced a "dragon" that helped you grow into a fresh understanding that your life is not really your own? If so, did it change your willingness to take risks in your life of faith?

8. Indiana Jones completed his quest with the help of an ancient how-to book. What aspects of Christian tradition and life help you handle the grace-quests you fear? Is there anything else you wish you had for the journey?

Chapter 10: Old Stone Church ~ love

1. If you had to express why you believe or don't believe in love, what would you share?

2. Are there special dangers to romantic love, or do the same dangers beset all kinds of love?

3. Concerning love, do you function from a standpoint of self-protection or self-sacrifice? Are you satisfied with the standpoint from which you operate? Do you believe that those around you are satisfied with your approach to love?

4. To what extent do you believe a person should graciously stand by another who is worthy of abandonment? To what extent do you desire others to graciously stand by you when you are worthy of abandonment?

5. What makes it possible for someone to gather another person's broken pieces and give them back in the right order? You might recall a time when someone has done that for you or when you

have done that for someone.

6. Growth in love with God and others depends on the risk of poking through the dark, the dead, the pain of what is past and what is longed for. In what ways are you willing to take that risk? Or not?

7. How do you feel about conceptualizing God as your Song of Songs true, passionate, intimate lover—maybe even praying to God using the words of the Song? Do you believe people might approach romantic love differently if they first understood their love with God in such terms?

8. As noted by Yancey, romantic love can teach us to split ourselves open to God. Yet romantic love isn't always a part of our lives. What other natural phenomena might be a springboard for experiencing God's gracious presence?

Chapter 11: Goldsworthy's Wall ~ sacrifice

1. What common ways has God worked in history to promote relationship, to keep it "front and center"? How do these works communicate grace?

2. Consider the relationships in your life. What challenges do they present? How are they opportunities to reveal God's nature and spread his grace?

3. Do you think Jesus came to earth more as master or as child? Does one role communicate grace more effectively than the other?

4. Which side of God do you most relate to: the master or the child? How might this affect your approach to relationships?

5. Do you ever view the ordinary relationships of life as obstacles to your fulfillment or achievements? How does Paul's statement in I Corinthians 13 speak to this view?

6. Do you agree or disagree with the thought that Christianity is primarily built on a set of relationships?

7. What is currently joining you to others: love and grace, or "pins and staples"? What would you like to do in light of this?

8. Would it change anything in your relationships if you thought of yourself as a gracious shepherd to others? How about if you thought of yourself as a builder, whose work God plans to set with precious stones?

Chapter 12: Clefts of the Rock ~ responsibility

1. Describe your privileges—your "patch of ground," your "scepter of influence," and those who are with you in "the clefts of the rock."

2. How have you been approaching each of these privileges? Have you been playing the hardworking shepherd or the bed-bound royal? If you have lapsed into laziness in certain areas, to what are you entrusting your vineyard—chance or servants of some sort?

3. Scripture suggests that those who do not act responsibly with their privileges suffer eternal loss. Does this motivate you to live your life responsibly?

4. To what extent are you motivated to act responsibly regarding your privileges based on a vision of abundance and delight?

5. How do you believe the temptation to be irresponsible functions? What lends it power?

6. Can the Sabbath teach us anything about the "empty path to fullness"? Does anything in your life serve as a good example of this phenomenon?

7. Is there really such a thing as true emptiness? Consider Jesus' act of "emptying himself" (see Philippians 2:7).

8. What kinds of discomforting discipline might help you trim past temptations? Is there anything inherent in the grace of Christ that might assist you?

Chapter 13: Olive Press ~ gratitude

1. When someone prays, "Thank you, Jesus, for paying the price for our sins," what response do you find within yourself?

2. Time can tempt us to forget why we need Jesus' sacrifice. On a practical level, how does this affect your spiritual life? Conversely, how might a keen sense of his gracious sacrifice affect it?

3. Take a moment to become a translator. What secret thoughts did you have today that were unkind, angry, lustful or impatient? If these thoughts were to translate into real marks on those around you, whom would they mark and how?

4. Now picture these marks being translated onto Jesus' flesh. What kind of response do you have as you watch the process?

5. What experience can you feel more keenly in your imagination—that of being lowered into a hole and stoned, or that of being raised and hung on a cross? Do you feel you are truly

deserving of either death? How does this affect your response to Jesus?

6. We often think of Gethsemane as the place where Jesus struggled to accept the pain of the cross. Does it change anything for you to consider Gethsemane as the place where Jesus met a guilty beloved and chose to set her free?

7. Ultimately, what do you believe motivated Jesus to go through with the pursuit of grace?

8. Consider the words "What I did not steal must I now restore?" How do they communicate the work of grace? Is there any way in which you might be called to restore what you have not stolen in the world?

Chapter 14: Forest Star ~ humility

1. The author dreamed of trying to fill a large stone enclosure with pebbles, perhaps as a kind of eventual monument. In what ways do these images speak to the potential effectiveness of trying to build glory for oneself?

2. Absalom used stone to build his memorial. Moses hit the rock. What are the materials you use to build honor for yourself? Are there positive aspects to building honor for oneself? Negative?

3. What does it mean, as Merton says, to be able to "be [oneself] at last"? Are there any ways you are living not as yourself?

4. Why do you think God brought water from the rock, if Moses called forth the miracle in such a way that brought glory to himself? What does this say about using ministry effectiveness as a measure of where we are spiritually?

5. Whose glory do you feel you are currently shining through your talents and position—your own or God's? How can you know if you are truly shining God's glory? What do you believe is the source of our desire to shine on our own?

6. In what ways are the "casualties great" when we promote our own glory in our various communities—marriage, family, friendships, town, church, world? How does this potentially differ from the work of grace?

7. Respond to the thought that your efforts to gain glory find their beginning and end in the Pit.

8. In what ways might God be trying to strand you on this side of the Promised Land? Or how has God done this in the past? Do you see this as an act of grace or disgrace? Why?

Chapter 15: Seedstone ~ healing

1. If someone searched the crumpled moments of your day, who would he really see?

2. Have your frailties ever discouraged you from trying to serve your spiritual community?

3. If the power of God is right within reach through the Holy Spirit, why do we sometimes botch our important jobs?

4. In what ways might it be important to go into exile when we fail? At what point should we seek to reenter community?

5. How much should we share about our failures to both secular and Christian communities? What purpose can our sharing serve?

6. Is there any value in a long journey of healing? In what areas do

you feel you've been sent into healing, perhaps even patched with mud, but are still waiting for light to dawn?

7. Does your community of believers give you a safe place to be born into healing? To celebrate healing that has already come through God's grace? Give examples.

8. Is there something you feel God still needs to burn to enable you to move forward in his grace with confidence and power? Ask him to do so today.

Chapter 16: Sugar Face ~ forgiveness

1. Define "forgiveness." What are its practical, observable fruits?

2. Remember an incident that was hard to forgive. What made it so? Conversely, remember a time when forgiveness came easy. What dynamics made it work out well?

3. What might remembering one's finiteness have to do with the ability to forgive?

4. Describe your understanding of an idol. Do you agree or disagree that unforgiveness can be a form of idolatry?

5. In what ways do you treat yourself royally in a situation where you can't seem to forgive someone? Describe specific ways you might be feeding yourself pure intentions while denying these to the other person.

6. If it is false to attribute all the good to ourselves and the failure to another, why do we sometimes do this?

7. What are the potential consequences now and eternally for bowing to unforgiveness?

8. If we feel we cannot forgive someone, what steps can we take? Is there anything about the grace of Jesus that could help us take these steps?

Chapter 17: Lava Rock ~ witness

1. Do you live with a desire to save others, spiritually or otherwise? How does this function positively or negatively? If you don't have this particular desire, how do you see it functioning either positively or negatively in someone else's life?

2. Do you ever compare yourself to someone who "easily" brings others to God? How does this comparison end up affecting you? If you are someone who seems to easily bring others to God, are you satisfied with how you're relating to those who don't?

3. Jesus called his followers to make disciples. What does this mean to you? Is it the same as being called to evangelize?

4. When it comes to telling others about the gospel, do you feel a sense of guilt or freedom? Explain.

5. If you were to conceive of yourself as a grace-bearer instead of someone who tries to save others, would this change anything in your life?

6. When Daniel first dealt with Nebuchadnezzar, the king ended up worshiping him, not God. Do you have relationships that are stuck at this level? What can you do to direct people beyond you, to the one who lights up your soul?

7. Consider that Nebuchadnezzar was alone when he finally turned to God. If God can bring people to himself without any human voice to mediate, why does he ever choose to involve us?

8. Do you have any relationships about which you feel hopeless—the way Daniel may have felt hopeless about Nebuchadnezzar's prospects for finding God? What encouragements can you take from remembering the king's path?

Chapter 18: Climbing ~ justice

1. What underlying thoughts or dynamics promote the "just is" view of the world? Do you agree that a person is enabled to participate more fully in justice work when she begins to find freedom from her own wounds?

2. Consider the ways you are free. Then respond to the statement, "The function of freedom is to free someone else."

3. Where are you in the process of your walk toward justice? Do you need awareness? Compassion? Boldness? Tools to be a problem solver? Consider how you might find what you need.

4. Are there certain pressures you might face if you decided to walk toward a justice view of the world? Do you fear seeming indelicate? Or inadequate?

5. Describe your view of Jesus. Is he meek and mild? Strong and assertive? What do you believe he incarnated? How might your view affect your relationship to issues of justice?

6. In what ways might justice be conflict? Can a person pursue justice completely free of confrontation?

7. Reflect on the concept of grace. In what ways does it seem related to power? Unrelated?

8. How do you feel about using power? What kinds of power do you

have to address justice concerns? (Consider various facets of your life, each of which involve some level of influence or power: economic, religious, educational, community and nation, organizational membership, media use, family, and so on.) How does your power in these areas relate to the power Jesus offers, as he offered to the disciples a multiplication of their foodstuffs in the desert?

Chapter 19: Roxaboxen ~ heaven

1. In your experience, do the dying move easily from life to death, or do they struggle?

2. Do you relate to the yearning for a lasting home, the search for a different country? Do you feel like a sojourner here? Explain.

3. Why do you think the Bible gives so little detail about heaven's nature and activities? If the Bible gave more detail, how would that affect you, if at all?

4. Do you expect others to face their deaths with readiness? Why or why not? What dynamics play into the way we deal with a dying friend?

5. Do you find comfort in Jesus' promise, "I go and prepare a place for you"? Do you think someone like Jesus would say such a thing if it weren't true? How would this statement be problematic if made by an ordinary person?

6. What do you imagine the place he's preparing will be like? (See Ezekiel 1; Revelation 21; 22:1-5.) In what ways might it be an embodiment of grace?

7. Consider your life's works. Which of these do you expect will follow you to heaven—what might still glow?

Chapter 20: Blood from a Stone ~ completion

1. How have you celebrated midlife birthdays? What might these celebrations reveal about your cultural views regarding aging?

2. Do you associate "development" with a person's later years? Why or why not? Explain.

3. Compare the challenge of growing older with the challenges people face in other seasons of life. What do these seasons share? How do they differ?

4. Should we be at all interested in reversing or preventing feebleness in old age? Does it have any spiritual implications?

5. We are called to care for the older generation, yet Langer's research suggests that premature care can cause premature degeneration. If you are involved in caring for an older person, what can you do to promote independence and resourcefulness for him or her? What kinds of difficulties might you face in doing so? What kinds of safeguards might ensure that such efforts remain balanced with the call to provide care?

6. Are certain kinds of ministry participation especially suited to those in the older generation? How might you encourage older-generation ministry in your circles?

7. What vision do you hold for your later years? How can you prepare now to be ready later? Among other things, consider some of the roles mentioned in the chapter: encouraging the young in their unique abilities, blessing their endeavors, embodying God's loving care.

8. What externals are you focusing on that will wither away? How might this affect you in your later years? What practical steps might you take to develop into a grace-bearer, now and in your future?

notes

Chapter 2: Christmas Coal

page 19   "If [Jesus] did what He said": Flannery O'Connor, "A Good Man Is Hard to Find," in *The Complete Stories of Flannery O'Connor* (New York: Farrar, Straus and Giroux, 1987), p. 132.

page 22   The Hebrew word here, *towla:* The word *towla* refers to both the color crimson and a particular type of worm, *Coccus ilicis*, as discussed at <http://cf.blueletterbible.org/lang/lexicon/lexicon.cfm?strongs=H08438&Version=kjv>.

Chapter 3: Tossed Treasure

page 25   "Accept the things": See "The Origin of Our Serenity Prayer" at <www.aahistory.com/prayer.html>.

page 28   She and her husband sheltered the apostle: Priscilla is noted by name, suggesting she had a good deal of influence in her life with Aquila. "The couple worked together as a team and . . . Aquila was unthreatened by his wife's strengths," says Lawrence O. Richards, ed., in *The Revell Bible Dictionary* (Old Tappan, N.J.: Fleming H. Revell, 1990), p. 817.

pages 28-29   Of the seven times: Ibid.

page 29   During Sukkot: Explanation of the Jewish festival of Sukkot is from Naomi Black, ed., *Celebration: The Book of Jewish Festivals* (Middle Village, N.Y.: Jonathan David, 1987), pp. 32-43.

page 30   This is the original language: Leland Ryken, James C. Wilhoit and Tremper Longman III, eds., *Dictionary of Biblical Imagery* (Downers Grove, Ill.: InterVarsity Press, 1998), p. 839.

Chapter 4: Heron Road

page 33   As a budding artist: Michael Elsohn Ross, *Salvador Dali and the Surrealists: Their Lives and Ideas* (Chicago: Chicago Review Press, 2003), pp. 18-19.

page 37   "The soles of [the prodigal's feet]": Henri Nouwen, *The Return of the Prodigal Son: A Story of Homecoming* (New York: Image, 1994), p. 46.

Chapter 5: Sword in the Stone

page 41   "Disney has a formula": Susan Konig, *Why Animals Sleep So Close to the Road, and Other Lies I Tell My Children* (New York: Thomas Dunne, 2005), p. xii.

page 41   To pull a sword from a stone: In legend, King Arthur's identity was first proved when he pulled a sword from a stone. As the sword was placed there by enchantment, only the true royal would be able to extract it.

page 43   Luther "regarded [the devil]": Jonathan Hill, *What Has Christianity Ever Done for Us?* (Downers Grove, Ill.: Inter-Varsity Press, 2005), p. 10.

Chapter 6: Howe's Cave

page 48   *Na'aseh v'nishma:* Lauren F. Winner, *Mudhouse Sabbath* (Brewster, Mass.: Paraclete, 2003), p. x.

page 51   If a Gentile wanted to convert: The mikvah is discussed
               in Leland Ryken, James C. Wilhoit and Tremper Long-
               man III, eds., *Dictionary of Biblical Imagery* (Downers Grove,
               Ill.: InterVarsity Press, 1998), pp. 72-73.

page 51   The term was associated: Lawrence O. Richards, *The Revell
               Bible Dictionary* (Old Tappan, N.J.: Fleming H. Revell,
               1990), p. 128.

Chapter 7: Palisade Cliffs

page 55   "Borderlands of belief": Philip Yancey, *Rumors of Another
               World: What on Earth Are We Missing?* (Grand Rapids:
               Zondervan, 2003), p. 9.

pages 56-57   "Something about the experiment": Michael Card, *A Fragile
               Stone* (Downers Grove, Ill.: InterVarsity Press, 2003), p. 52.

page 57   When we see Jesus: Ibid., p. 73.

page 57   I recently read a memoir: Julia Scheeres, *Jesus Land: A Mem-
               oir* (New York: Counterpoint, 2005).

Chapter 8: Holding Pfaltzgraff

page 60   The isolation of lepers in Europe: This description is taken
               from Jeanette Farrell, *Invisible Enemies: Stories of Infectious Disease*
               (New York: Farrar, Straus and Giroux, 1998), pp. 55-56.

page 61   Susan Opotow, at the University of Massachusetts Bos-
               ton: This research was discussed in a phone conversation
               with Susan Opotow on May 27, 2006.

page 64   The original language: Discussed in Leland Ryken, James C.
               Wilhoit and Tremper Longman III, eds., *Dictionary of Bibli-
               cal Imagery* (Downers Grove, Ill.: InterVarsity Press, 1998),
               p. 839.

Chapter 9: Indiana Jones

page 69   The original language used: Discussed in Leland Ryken, James C. Wilhoit and Tremper Longman III, eds., *Dictionary of Biblical Imagery* (Downers Grove, Ill.: InterVarsity Press, 1998), p. 217.

page 71   Or possibly the airy laryngeal pouch: Discussed in Lawrence O. Richards, *The Revell Bible Dictionary* (Old Tappan, N.J.: Fleming H. Revell, 1990), p. 579.

Chapter 10: Old Stone Church

page 75   "She is a friend of my mind": Toni Morrison, *Beloved* (New York: Alfred A. Knopf, 1987), pp. 272-73.

page 76   The song lyrics are by Michael Card and Scott Brasher from *The Way of Wisdom* ©1990, Sparrow Records.

page 77   Iain Provan suggests: Iain Provan, *The New Application Commentary: Ecclesiastes/Song of Songs* (Grand Rapids: Zondervan, 2001), pp. 266-370.

page 78   Philip Yancey credits: Philip Yancey, *Rumors of Another World: What on Earth Are We Missing?* (Grand Rapids: Zondervan, 2003), pp. 88-89.

Chapter 11: Goldsworthy's Wall

page 81   When I encounter a piece: Goldsworthy's stone wall described here is at Storm King Art Center in Mountainville, New York.

page 83   "God communicate[s] himself": Mark Strom, *Reframing Paul: Conversations in Grace and Community* (Downers Grove, Ill.: InterVarsity Press, 2000), p. 174.

pages 85-86 "Oh, there will be a day": Martin Luther King Jr., "The Three Dimensions of a Complete Life," in *A Knock at Mid-*

night: Inspiration from the Great Sermons of Reverend Martin Luther King, Jr., ed. Clayborne Carson and Peter Holloran (New York: Intellectual Properties Management with Warner Books, 1998), pp. 130-31.

Chapter 12: Clefts of the Rock

pages 92-93   "The line of words": Annie Dillard, "The Writing Life," in *Three by Annie Dillard* (New York: Perennial, 2001), pp. 549-50.

pages 93-94   "Where you got your seeds": Demi, *The Empty Pot* (New York: Henry Holt, 1990), pp. 29-30.

Chapter 13: Olive Press

page 95   Guns "exchang[e] shatter prayers"; a "red stain blossoms": Yasmina Khadra, *The Swallows of Kabul,* trans. John Cullen (New York: Doubleday, 2002), p. 1.

Chapter 14: Forest Star

page 104   "Someone accused me": Thomas Merton, *A Year with Thomas Merton: Daily Meditations from His Journals,* ed. Jonathan Montaldo (New York: HarperSanFrancisco, 2004), p. 7.

Chapter 15: Seedstone

page 109   I learned about this great American freedom: Elizabeth Royte, *Garbage Land: On the Secret Trail of Trash* (New York: Little, Brown, 2005), p. 35.

page 112   "My son goes down": Madeleine L'Engle, "Fire by Fire," in *The Weather of the Heart* (Wheaton, Ill.: Harold Shaw, 1978). Used by permission.

page 113   "We need more creative visionaries": Makoto Fujimura,

"Planting Seedlings in Stone: Art in New York City," *Comment* 25 (December 2, 2005) <www.wrf.ca/Comment/article.cfm?ID=151>.

page 113   There's a wonderful children's book: Helen Ward, *The Tin Forest* (New York: Dutton Children's Books, 2001).

Chapter 16: Sugar Face

pages 119-20 I also considered: The inspiration of idols is discussed in Leland Ryken, James C. Wilhoit and Tremper Longman III, eds., *Dictionary of Biblical Imagery* (Downers Grove, Ill.: InterVarsity Press, 1998), p. 416.

page 120   The term *idol* can simply mean "a falsehood": Lawrence O. Richards, *The Revell Bible Dictionary* (Old Tappan, N.J.: Fleming H. Revell, 1990), p. 510.

Chapter 17: Lava Rock

pages 123-24 "I saw a bubble": Marilynne Robinson, *Gilead* (New York: Farrar, Straus and Giroux, 2004), p. 9.

Chapter 18: Climbing

page 127   "The function of freedom": Toni Morrison, quoted by Anne Lamott in *Bird by Bird: Some Instructions on Writing and Life* (New York: Pantheon, 1994), p. 193.

page 128   "It's a long way to Nairobi": Quoted in Frances Moore Lappe and Anna Lappe, *Hope's Edge: The New Diet for a Small Planet* (New York: Putnam, 2002), p. 181.

page 131   Paul Coughlin speculates: Paul Coughlin, quoted by Camerin Courtney in "No More Christian Nice Guy," *Today's Christian Woman* (March/April 2006): 39.

pages 131-32 It means "straightness": Discussed by I. Howard Marshall, A. R. Millard, J. I. Packer and D. J. Wiseman, *New Bible Dictionary*, 3rd. ed. (Leicester, U.K.: Inter-Varsity Press, 1996), p. 635.

page 132   To borrow a book title: Stuart Hampshire, *Justice Is Conflict* (Princeton, N.J.: Princeton University Press, 2000).

Chapter 19: Roxaboxen

page 133   A place called Roxaboxen: Alice McLerran, *Roxaboxen* (New York: Lothrop, Lee & Shepard, 1991).

page 135   "It had brought me": Henri J. M. Nouwen, *The Return of the Prodigal Son: A Story of Homecoming*, Image Books ed. (New York: Doubleday, 1992), p. 5.

page 135   "It doesn't seem to be here": Annie Dillard, *Teaching a Stone to Talk: Expeditions and Encounters* (New York: HarperPerennial, 1982), p. 149.

page 137   "Once there was a little bunny": Margaret Wise Brown, *The Runaway Bunny* (New York: Harper & Row, 1942), pp. 1-3, 15.

page 138   Almanzo prepares a new home: Laura Ingalls Wilder, *These Happy Golden Years* (New York: Harper, 1953).

Chapter 20: Blood from a Stone

page 141   We "rarely [use] the term *development*": Ellen J. Langer, *Mindfulness* (Reading, Mass.: Addison-Wesley, 1989), p. 96.

page 141   What Langer found: Ibid., pp. 81-113.

pages 141-42 "Most of the arbitrary limits": Ibid., p. 98.

page 144   "Old trees, hospitable": Bill McConnell, "Community Life." Used by permission.

page 146   Our contentment is "based on externals": Darrell L. Bock, *The NIV Application Commentary: Luke* (Grand Rapids: Zondervan, 1996), p. 97.